New Kid in School

USING LITERATURE TO HELP CHILDREN IN TRANSITION

New Kid in School

Using Literature to Help Children in Transition

Debra Rader
Linda Harris Sittig

Teachers College
Columbia University
New York and London

Published by Teachers College Press, 1234 Amsterdam Avenue, New York, NY 10027

Library of Congress Cataloging-in-Publication Data

Rader, Debra.
    New kid in school : using literature to help children in transition / Debra Rader, Linda Harris Sittig.
        p. cm.
    Includes bibliographical references and index.
    ISBN 0-8077-4315-1 (cloth) — ISBN 0-8077-4314-3 (pbk.)
        1. Children's literature—Study and teaching (Elementary) 2. Children—Books and reading. 3. Moving, Household—Juvenile literature—History and criticism. 4. Multicultural education. I. Sittig, Linda Harris. II. Title.

    LB1575.R33 2003
    372.64'044—dc21   2002038432

ISBN 0-8077-4314-3 (paper)
ISBN 0-8077-4315-1 (cloth)

Printed on acid-free paper

Manufactured in the United States of America

10   09   08   07   06   05   04   03   8   7   6   5   4   3   2   1

Contents

Foreword   *Robert R. Spillane*   vii

Acknowledgments   ix

Introduction   xi

1   Background of the Book   1
Why Did We Write This Book?   1
Background on Transition and Mobility   2
Using This Book   4
Tips for Teachers   6

2   The Common Experience of Mobility   13
A New Home for Tiger by Joan Stimson   16
Sarah, Plain and Tall by Patricia MacLachlan   19
Painted Words and Spoken Memories by Aliki   24
Gila Monsters Meet You at the Airport by Marjorie Weinman Sharmat   29
Bloomability by Sharon Creech   33

3   The Process of Transition   41
Alexander, Who's Not (Do you hear me? I mean it!) Going to Move
   by Judith Viorst   47
Dandelions by Eve Bunting   51
Scrumpy by Elizabeth Dale   55
We Are Best Friends by Aliki   58
In the Year of the Boar and Jackie Robinson by Bette Bao Lord   61

4   Personal and Cultural Identity   68
Stellaluna by Janell Cannon   72
Grandfather's Journey by Allen Say   76
When I Was Young in the Mountains by Cynthia Rylant   79
little blue and little yellow by Leo Lionni   81
Seedfolks by Paul Fleischman   83

5   **Friendships and Relationships**   **90**
        Best Friends Together Again by Aliki   93
        Mrs. Katz and Tush by Patricia Polacco   96
        Amber Brown is Not a Crayon by Paula Danziger   99
        The Kid in the Red Jacket by Barbara Park   103
        Beyond the Mango Tree by Amy Bronwen Zemser   107

6   **Problem-Solving Skills**   **114**
        Chicken Sunday by Patricia Polacco   117
        Chrysanthemum by Kevin Henkes   121
        Ira Says Goodbye by Bernard Waber   124
        Molly's Pilgrim by Barbara Cohen   128
        The Lotus Seed by Sherry Garland   131

7   **Moving Back**   **136**
        When Africa Was Home by Karen Lynn Williams   141
        Tea With Milk by Allen Say   146
        Going Home by Eve Bunting   150
        The Trip Back Home by Janet S. Wong   154
        "They Don't Do Math in Texas" in *If You're Not Here, Please
            Raise Your Hand* by Kalli Dakos   156

Appendix A   Cross-Referenced Literature and Transition Links   161
Appendix B   Children's Literature Resources   163
Appendix C   Suggested Resources Related to Transition   165
Appendix D   Suggested Transition Activities   167
Appendix E   Approaches to Transition   169
Appendix F   Tips for Parents   171

References   175
Index   177
About the Authors   185

Foreword

Relocation brings significant changes and can be a source of great stress for children. As a former superintendent of several school districts in the United States with highly mobile populations, and in my current work with overseas schools, I have become well aware of the transition issues facing children who move both domestically and internationally, and the need to address those issues.

Educators are becoming increasingly concerned about the emotional well-being of children, and schools can play an important role in addressing transition issues with their students.

Research confirms that mobile children have particular needs. This book is unique in that it builds on research in the field of mobility, and bridges theory and practice to provide educators with viable and inspired ways to meet the particular needs of children in transition. *New Kid in School: Using Literature to Help Children in Transition* is an excellent professional resource that provides educators with ideas and strategies they can use to teach children about transitions and help them develop skills to effectively manage the many changes involved in moving.

The strength of this book is that the materials are designed for use by educators working in all primary schools—public, independent, and international—worldwide. They are easy to use in the classroom and can be naturally integrated into the existing curriculum in any school. The authors have chosen quality children's literature as a springboard for learning about transitions and have developed excellent follow-up activities and creative ideas for cross-curricular connections.

Debra Rader and Linda Sittig have had the educational vision to see the need to develop transition education materials that can benefit all children. Both authors bring tremendous expertise to this project. They have extensive experience working with mobile student populations and are accomplished educators. Linda Sittig has taught as a reading specialist for the past 30 years in two school districts with high mobility rates in the United States. Her expertise is in using literature to adapt the curriculum to fit the special needs of students, including students who are making the transition to a new country and for whom English is not their primary language. Debra Rader was the primary and middle school principal at Southbank International School Kensington in London, England. She has worked with mobile children and their families in public, independent, and international schools, and has taught at the primary and middle school levels both in the United States and abroad. The experiences of these two educators complement each other, and give them a profound understanding of transition and mobility.

Transition education is an exciting new concept, and I welcome this professional resource as a much-needed contribution to the field of education and to the lives of children.

Robert R. Spillane, Ph.D.
Regional Education Officer
Office of Overseas Schools
U.S. Department of State
Former Superintendent of Boston and Fairfax County Public Schools

Acknowledgments

From Debra Rader

I am grateful to all of the mobile children and families I have met and worked with who have taught me so very much about the experience of transition.

This book would not be possible without the enormous support and encouragement of many individuals whose enthusiasm and belief in the project was constant.

Special thanks go to David Pollock for his leadership in the field of transition and international mobility, and for his enthusiastic support of this resource. His feedback on sections of the manuscript was most valuable and encouraging.

I am indebted to my friend and colleague Mary Langford for her valuable contributions during our many conversations about transition. She gave generously of her time and read through the manuscript with a critical eye. As a Third Culture Kid herself, she gave insights and suggestions that were greatly appreciated.

I would particularly like to thank my colleague and friend Linda Erickson for sharing her tremendous love and knowledge of children's literature.

I am also deeply appreciative of the support and encouragement of Beckett Ender, Mary Hannert, Debbie Howe, Norma McCaig, and Richard Pearce.

Very special thanks also go to Tony Denbeigh for the generous contribution of his time, patience, and computer expertise.

A very special thank-you goes to my husband, Jim, for his unfailing support and encouragement throughout the writing of this book and for his interest in the work. Also for making those countless cups of tea!

Last, but not least, I would like to thank Brian Ellerbeck and the staff at Teachers College Press for having the vision to support such an important topic and for their endorsement of this project.

From Linda Harris Sittig

I want to acknowledge the efforts of Georgia McGuire and Harriette Best for turning a public school into a multicultural community where every child feels welcome, and for hiring me to teach on their staff.

I feel a need to thank the children of Freedom Hill Elementary School and the 46 countries they represent, for teaching me the true meaning of transition and mobility.

Last, but not least, I thank my husband, Jim, who truly is the wind beneath my wings.

Introduction

Our world is an increasingly mobile place with families moving more often than ever before. While a move to a new city, state, or country can be very exciting, it is not without its challenges! There are tremendous benefits to experiencing life in a new place. However, a move can also be confusing and worrisome for children as they are faced with a new home, a new school, a new neighborhood, and possibly a new culture and language all at once.

Transition education provides children with the knowledge and skills to successfully manage transitions while affirming and celebrating their unique experiences and backgrounds. Educators have a significant influence on the lives of children and are therefore in a prime position to explore transition issues in the classroom. Through transition education, children can learn to appreciate and value the new experiences they encounter and the skills they have learned as a result of their mobility. Ultimately, transition education helps them to face change with confidence and enthusiasm.

Transition education is another thread that can be easily woven into the tapestry of the existing curriculum in any school. This book provides classroom and specialist teachers for grades K–5 with a model for transition education and background information on the topic of transition and mobility. It also offers lesson plans that include suggested activities and strategies they can use to help children learn more about transition, develop a stronger sense of self-awareness, and gain an appreciation of new places and other cultures.

Most children are affected by transition in some way during their lives. If they do not move, it is likely that at some point a friend, relative, or classmate will move. The children left behind also experience transition adjustments. This book can be used to help all children who experience transition, whether they move within their own country or abroad, including immigrant and refugee children. Transition education is not only timely, it is essential as we prepare children for life in a diverse and fast-changing world such as ours.

New Kid in School

USING LITERATURE TO HELP CHILDREN IN TRANSITION

Chapter 1

Background of the Book

WHY DID WE WRITE THIS BOOK?

It was through our work with mobile children and their families that we first became interested in the field of transition and student mobility. We saw children and their parents going through the stresses associated with adapting to a new environment, and we became increasingly aware of the issues they faced during the process of relocation, particularly when moving to another country and culture. We saw them struggling with a new language, confused by a new culture, and worried about finding a place for themselves in their new community.

We found that transition support was provided sporadically for expatriate families, usually in the form of cross-cultural training or relocation seminars for the working parent and accompanying spouse. However, there was little support available for children. Immigrant and refugee families received little if any assistance in their adjustment to a new country and culture.

While research confirmed that mobile children had particular social and emotional needs, strategies and resource tools to meet those needs were lacking. Many schools were beginning to recognize that they had a role and responsibility to support their students and families through making the transition to their community and began to implement programs and transition activities to facilitate their arrival and departure. We saw there was a particular need to provide teachers with ideas and materials that go beyond transition activities and help children learn about the experience of transition and develop essential life skills.

As we developed a viable concept of transition education, we found natural links for incorporating transition-related topics into existing curricula at every turn. The result was the development of this book.

BACKGROUND ON TRANSITION AND MOBILITY

Transition is defined in the dictionary as a change from one state or stage to another, or the period of time during which something changes. This term has been used to describe a wide range of life experiences; however, for the purpose of this book, transition refers to the changes one experiences when moving from one location to another.

John and Ruth Useem, social scientists from Michigan State University, began their research on mobility in the 1950s when they traveled to India to study expatriate families living there. They discovered that these families lived in expatriate communities and were not a part of the host culture nor of their home culture, but of a "third culture" with other expatriates of similar experience who were living in and relating to a culture other than their own.

Ruth Useem (1976) later studied young adults who returned to the United States to attend university after living abroad. She found that they had different characteristics than their peers who had grown up in the United States, and that they experienced a common reaction to returning to their passport country. She published her research findings and described these children as "Third Culture Kids" or TCKs.

According to David Pollock (1999), Useem has broadened the definition of the third culture to describe the lifestyle in which individuals from one culture are in the process of relating to another one. She has also broadened the term *TCK* to include all children who accompany their parents to another society. While there are certain characteristics that are particular to children who are internationally mobile, immigrant and refugee children and children who are domestically mobile share many of the same characteristics.

Pollock, who is a leading authority in the field of transition and international mobility, defines the Third Culture Kid as follows:

> A Third Culture Kid (TCK) is a person who has spent a significant part of his or her developmental years outside the parents' culture. The TCK builds relationships to all of the cultures, while not having full ownership in any. Although elements from each culture are assimilated into the TCK's life experiences, the sense of belonging is in relationship to others of similar background. (Pollock & Van Reken, 1999, p. 19)

Norma McCaig (1992) later developed the term *global nomad* to describe these children, and both terms are now used interchangeably.

Pollock & Van Reken (1999) has identified the following stages of the process of transition: involvement, leaving, transition, entering, and reinvolvement, which are described in Chapter 3, "The Process of Transition." Through his extensive work with internationally mobile children and their families, he has identified characteristics that present both benefits and challenges to individuals who have lived abroad, including an expanded view of the world, adaptability, cross-cultural skills, social skills, observational skills, linguistic skills, confused loyalties, a sense of rootlessness and restlessness, a lack of true identity, and unresolved grief. Research of adult TCKs, ages 25–90, confirmed that these characteristics were lifelong (Useem & Cottrell, 1996). Pollock advocates support for TCKs to help them develop to their full potential and benefit from the richness of their international experience.

While much of the research has been conducted with international school children, it is recognized that children who move within the same country face significant challenges as well. Jasper (2000) states that when children move they lose a sense of place in the local culture and the friendships that give them a sense of belonging. Their identity is affected and the experience can be extremely stressful. In Jason (1992) researchers in the United States found that children who move face significant transition issues socially, emotionally, and academically, and schools must develop a plan to address them.

During the past 20 years a wide range of articles have been appearing in professional journals that address the impact of mobility on the lives of children and families domestically as well as abroad. An extensive literature list is provided in Langford (1999); Wertsch (1991) has also written about the effects of mobility on children in military families in the United States and abroad.

Useem (1976) found that children growing up outside of their home country shared unique characteristics. She was concerned, however, that few educators were aware of this. Mary Langford (1998) shared the same concerns and conducted research among international school educators and administrators. She asked, "What is it that educators understand about global nomads and what are international schools doing to accommodate their needs?" Hers is the first quantitative data that shows that educators do see internationally mobile children as having unique characteristics and qualities, as well as particular academic, social, and emotional needs. Educators also thought that international schools have a role in meeting those needs. It logically follows that schools everywhere have a responsibility to meet the needs of their mobile populations.

Based on the issues facing mobile children and the desire to help teachers gain an understanding of what transition education encompasses, Debra Rader developed the model for Transition Education shown in Figure 1.1. This model comprehensively addresses and integrates the many dimen-

FIGURE 1.1. A Model of Transition Education (© Debra J. Rader, Educational Consultant, November 1998)

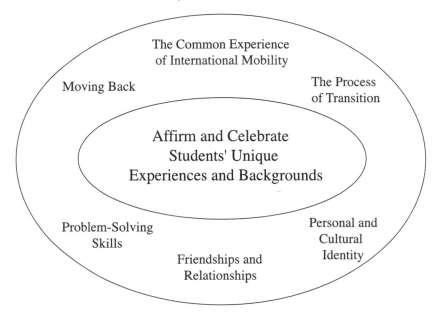

sions of the transition experience. Affirming and celebrating students' unique experiences and backgrounds lie at the heart of the model. It is then comprised of the following six components: the Common Experience of Mobility, the Process of Transition, Personal and Cultural Identity, Friendships and Relationships, Problem-Solving Skills, and Moving Back. Each component addresses important concepts and objectives to help children develop the knowledge and skills to successfully manage the transitions involved in moving to a new location.

McKillop-Ostrom (2000) identifies transition education as an important component of transition programming in international schools. Schaetti (1998) advocates establishing transition resource teams to provide the transition support in school, of which transition education is a part.

The model forms the basis for this resource book and provides practical solutions that are adaptable to any primary or elementary curriculum.

USING THIS BOOK

New Kid in School is divided into six main chapters, each reflecting a component of the transition education model and the transition issues addressed within each component. Within each chapter, the following features will be found:

- An introduction to the component of transition education being addressed
- The concepts to be presented and explored
- Lesson plans using children's literature to introduce the concepts, including learning objectives, suggestions for introducing the books, discussion questions, and additional follow-up activities
- Ideas for cross-curricular connections

This book is designed so that transition education can be easily integrated into your curriculum. It is suggested that you first make yourself aware of the transition issues facing mobile children by reading through the background on transition and mobility, tips for teachers, the introduction, and concepts presented in each chapter. You are encouraged to customize the use of these materials for the makeup of your particular class, the grade level you teach, and your students' particular needs. In each chapter, examples are provided for children moving both domestically and internationally. Attention is also given to children who experience a high degree of mobility, immigrant and refugee children, and children who are not mobile.

We recommend beginning with Chapters 2 and 3, "The Common Experience of Mobility" and "The Process of Transition," as these are central to transition education and seen as prerequisites for exploring other transition issues. The remaining components can then be addressed in any order you wish. You do not need to use all of the books or activities suggested in a chapter before you move on. In fact, it is best if you revisit the different transition issues from time to time. Transition education is more than facilitating the arrival and departure of students, and should be ongoing throughout the school year. This shows that transition issues are valued and respected, and seen as important.

In addition to providing children with the knowledge and skills to successfully manage transitions, there are several adjuncts to transition education.

- While the skills developed in transition education are framed within the context of mobility, they are life skills that can be used to face all changes.
- Cross-cultural skills such as cross-cultural awareness, sensitivity, adaptation, and communication are interwoven in the components of transition education. These are essential skills for life in a diverse society and

go beyond fostering tolerance to encourage an interest in and an appreciation, respect, and acceptance of other cultures.

- Transition education encourages the development of empathy and compassion as children explore the experiences and feelings associated with moving and being left behind.
- Transition education is an important part of parent education as most children are affected by transition in some way during their lives. Parents often look to the school for guidance in addressing issues affecting their children, and transition education provides educators with ideas and strategies they can share with parents.

Children's literature is an excellent vehicle for introducing transition issues and teaching life skills. While we have selected books for each component, you will find that the literature suggested often relates to more than one component of the transition education model and can be used to address many issues. The books are therefore cross-referenced in the chart in Appendix A and Transition Education Links are included in each lesson plan.

Once you become familiar with the transition issues associated with mobility, you are likely to see the natural links that exist in different subject areas in your curriculum. Experiment! Have fun exploring other ways you can integrate transition education into the subjects studied and projects undertaken in your classroom! We also encourage you to think of ways to include transition education in your future curriculum planning and development and in the new materials you select.

TIPS FOR TEACHERS

There is much you can do to create a classroom environment that honors and respects the children in your care and acknowledges the impact transition has on their lives. We encourage you to address transition education directly through the academic curriculum, indirectly through modeling and the examples you use, and in the ways you structure the classroom.

Direct Ways to Address Transition Education

- Resources and materials you use
- Activities and assignments
- Project work
- Class discussions

The lesson plans in this book provide a wealth of ideas for your use, but we hope they will inspire you to develop many of your own. Look for opportunities to incorporate your students' backgrounds, knowledge, and experiences into class discussions, projects, and assignments in different subject areas.

Make sure that the materials you select and display in your classroom reflect the cultures of the children you teach and others in the school. Include a wide variety of books, both fiction and nonfiction, from other countries in your classroom library. Help establish and maintain a resource library in your school. Include a picture library with photographs of artifacts, celebrations, food, clothing, art, dance, music, and customs of other cultures.

Be sure to include materials and projects in your curriculum that enable your students from other countries to learn about the host culture as well.

Indirect Ways to Address Transition Education

- *Modeling*

Model your own interest in and value of other cultures. Demonstrate a healthy curiosity about the cultures represented in your classroom and school and in the whole world.

- *Varying teaching strategies*

Vary your teaching strategies to address the different learning styles students bring to the classroom. Some of these may be due to their different cultures. While some of the children in your class may have come from child-centered programs, others may have come from more traditional schools. In child-centered classrooms children are encouraged to take an active role in their own learning, whereas traditional classrooms are more teacher directed, highly structured learning environments. These differences can affect the nature of teacher-student relationships and determine how formal or informal they may be. It is important to recognize that children may be reluctant to engage in activities that are seen as disrespectful in their own culture. For example, answering questions in class or performing publicly may be deeply embarrassing for some children. A wide range of activities will ensure that all children are engaged in something familiar, which can help ease their stress.

- *Making references to transition-related experiences*

The thread of transition education can be kept alive by referring to transition-related issues in the context of another lesson. For example, Nancy Walker wrote a beautiful Native American poem in her book *Spiritwalker*. It is called "Never Shall I Leave."

Never shall I leave the places that I love
Never shall they go from my heart
Even though my eyes are somewhere else.

You might read this poem as part of your study of Native Americans and simply say, "Many of you may feel this way about places you have lived and loved." In this way, your students' experience is acknowledged and you can continue with your curriculum plans.

• *Using examples in instruction*

Use your students' backgrounds or transition-related experiences in the context of another lesson. If you are teaching map skills, for example, you could say, "Kaori is visiting her family in Japan. What direction would she travel to get there?" In this way you are teaching the concept of direction while affirming your student's background.

Ways to Structure the Classroom

• *Learning activities*

Use a variety of small group, large group, and individual activities.

• *Seating*

Although you cannot force friendships, you can facilitate relationships by providing opportunities for your students to work together and get to know each other. Consider assigning buddies or pairing students for project work. Thoughtful consideration to assigning seats can also help foster relationships between students.

• *Classroom programs*

Consider implementing a "Super Star" or "VIP of the Week" program that showcases each child. This is a wonderful way to celebrate every student and help classmates learn about each other. Establishing a class post office is another idea that could complement a class writing project where children keep in touch with friends who have moved away.

• *Building a sense of community*

Consider ways to set a positive tone in your classroom and create an atmosphere of acceptance and appreciation. Begin the year with an "Interest Inventory" to learn more about your students. This is a personal survey that includes questions about family, hobbies, favorite books, subjects or animals, the child's interests, and what they want to learn. It is a wonderful way to gain information about your students to help you connect with them. You might have regular class meetings, write back and forth to your students in a dialogue journal, or keep a class "Awareness Log" in which you and the children record acts of kindness and thoughtfulness in your classroom.

The following are basic guidelines for working with mobile children and their families. Additional suggestions are found in the subsequent chapters.

Guidelines for Working with Mobile Families

• Recognize that if teachers and administrators value and respect transition issues, students also will see them as important.
• Transition education should have a positive effect; don't overplay or underplay transition issues, but look for natural links that exist within your curriculum.
• Be careful not to assume you know how others feel; let them tell you.
• Consider sharing your own experiences of mobility and transition with your students and their families. If you have recently moved yourself, be aware of where you are in the process of transition.
• Recognize that as children and their families adjust to living in another culture, they are likely to experience some degree of culture shock. This may be particularly difficult for some children, and it is important to be aware of signs of stress. In more extreme cases, these may include anxiety, irritability, aggressiveness, withdrawal, physical ailments, confusion or depression. While experiencing culture shock is normal for the children, you may need to engage the help of your principal, the school counselor, or an outside professional if the symptoms persist for a prolonged period of time.
• Some children may move under traumatic circumstances such as political upheaval or natural disasters. Be aware that returning to the place they lived before may not be possible. Separation from family, friends, and neighbors may be particularly painful.

Cultural Differences

• Learn to pronounce your students' and their parents' names correctly.
• Be open to learning about cultural differences, and do not expect your students to respond to situations in the same way you do. Assist them with adapting to a new culture while valuing their own culture or cultures.
• Be aware of your own biases and reactions to cultural differences.
• Model sensitivity to cultural differences and be aware and respectful of differences with physical contact, communication, food, health, and religious issues.
• You may find there are situations where you need to explain to students from different cultural backgrounds that this is the way things are done in your school.

• Many children adapt to the school culture while at school and switch back to their family culture at home. Sometimes the exposure to different values and behaviors at school can cause conflict between parents and their children. You may find yourself in the position of mediating between students and their parents when cultural differences arise.

• Be respectful of cultural differences, but address cultural practices that may conflict with your own or your country's values and morality. Deal with each situation individually, and enlist the help of your school principal.

• As a result of cultural differences, your students may view certain practices negatively. Recognize that they are trying to be "good" according to their own cultural practices.

Working with Children

• Get to know more about your students. Find out about their backgrounds and life experiences, prior school experiences, and who they are as individuals.

• Establish a sense of community in your classroom. While this is important in any school, it is of paramount importance in schools serving mobile students. This helps give children a sense of security at a time that can be particularly stressful.

• Acknowledge and validate the feelings and experiences of your students as they go through the transition process. Don't worry about having all the answers. Engage the help of school counselors and mental health professionals if necessary.

• Some students may deny experiencing any negative feelings, which is often a defense for feelings of vulnerability.

• Help your students engage in the life of the school. Encourage them to participate in extracurricular activities that interest them, such as art, music, or sports, and to explore the opportunities for joining after-school activities. Help them identify appealing community-based activities as well. This is particularly important for highly mobile children since it is an excellent way for children to engage with the local community and perhaps form some friendships that will be less transient.

• Children in your classes will probably arrive having widely different school experiences and educational backgrounds. It is therefore essential to assess your students carefully upon arrival and throughout the year to make sure that any educational gaps are addressed.

• It is important to differentiate instruction for all of your students to address the diverse learning needs present in your classroom.

• If you have children who leave during the school year, continue to display their work in your permanent class displays to let the other students know they are remembered even though they have moved on. This lets all children know they will not be forgotten if they leave.

• Provide opportunities for children to plan an activity for the future and carry out that plan. Many children who are mobile may find it difficult to plan ahead and become reluctant to do so, as their plans are often disrupted by an unexpected move.

• Remember that children may move at any point during the year. Be prepared to welcome students throughout the year and help them engage in the life of the classroom and the life of the school.

• It is important to note that children can leave the school community just as quickly as they came, sometimes without the opportunity to say good-bye. This is very difficult for both the child who is leaving and the children who are left behind. Look for ways to help all of the children through the transition such as writing good-bye notes to the student after he or she has left, or sending on a class project you may have been working on or a school yearbook.

Working with Parents

• As a child's teacher you will have a key role in helping the entire family adjust to the new school and culture, or prepare for departure. Parents often look to the school for advice and guidance on issues regarding their children. There is much you can do to help educate parents about the transition issues affecting their children as well as themselves. You may well find yourself in the position of helping a parent to settle in.

• Cultural differences may cause parents to feel frustrated or confused when they don't understand the procedures in a school. Be respectful and sensitive, and take them seriously.

• Help parents understand that they may see their child's cultural identity differently than their child does. They may impose an identity on their child which may not be the way the child sees him- or herself.

• Consider opportunities to involve parents in the sharing of projects and published student work related to transition issues. This provides the family with a shared experience about transition.

Professional Development

• Learn about the experiences of transition and international and domestic mobility by reading professional literature and attending seminars on the topic.

• Consider initiating the formation of a Transition Resource Team at your school to plan and coordinate transition programming. Include colleagues—administrators as well as fellow teachers—parents, and students on the team.

Tips for Working with Second Language Learners

Second language children face the challenge of learning English while at the same time adapting to a new culture. There is much you can do to ease the process of adjustment.

- Learn greetings and how to speak a few words in the child's native language, and teach your students to do so as well.
- Label items in the classroom in the child's language and in English.
- Establish clear routines in your classroom and incorporate teaching strategies to help facilitate second language learning for your students.
- Remember that in addition to modifying class work, you may need to give some thought to appropriate homework assignments.
- The importance of maintaining the home language and culture has long been documented by research. Some students are so eager to fit in with their peers, however, that they resist continuing to learn their mother tongue. You can play a positive role in helping your students to see the value of maintaining their own language as well as acquiring the new one.

In conclusion, by providing support and understanding, you can help maximize the benefits and ease the challenges of an international or domestic move for the children and families you work with.

Chapter 2

The Common Experience of Mobility

Transition is part of our human experience. Throughout history, people have been moving and adapting to new environments. As human beings, we have a need to belong to a community, and people who move to new places often share some of the same experiences. There are several worries and concerns that seem to be most common. People wonder if they will fit in with the new community. They worry about leaving old friends and whether they will make new ones. They also question where home is, miss people and places that were special to them, and experience a sense of loss at having to leave them behind. These concerns become more acute when moving to a city, state, or country where the culture or language is significantly different from what they have experienced before.

While moving is difficult for everyone, it is particularly stressful for children. They lose their sense of security and may feel disoriented when their routine is disrupted and all that is familiar is taken away. Young children, ages 3–6, are particularly affected by a move. Their understanding at this stage is quite literal, and it is hard for them to imagine beforehand a new home and their new room. Young children may have worries such as "Will I still be me in the new place?" and "Will my toys and bed come with us?"

It is important to establish a balance between affirming your students' past experiences and focusing on helping them adjust to the new place. Children need to have opportunities to share their backgrounds in a way that honors and respects their past as an important part of who they are. This contributes to building a sense of community, which is essential for all children, especially those in transition. In most schools, children are expected to quickly adapt to the new culture and put their previous experiences behind them. There is an unspoken understanding that they shouldn't talk too much about where they have been because others won't be able to relate to it, may find it boring, may think they don't like the new place, or think they are bragging. Their past experiences are therefore largely ignored. It is important for children to be truly seen and known by their teachers and classmates, and for educators to take an interest in who their students are and where they have been. This affirms their sense of self and gives them a sense of security that will help them settle into the new place.

Educators have an important role to play in helping children develop the understanding and skills necessary to ease the transitions of a move and in helping facilitate their adjustment to the new place. It is important to address the concerns children have and to let them know that others share their feelings. Acknowledging their feelings and experiences is a powerful intervention in itself.

As you explore these transition experiences with your students, remember that these are tendencies and no two people are alike. Be willing to listen to your students and learn from them. They can teach you a great deal about the experience of mobility and about themselves as individuals.

CONCEPTS FEATURED IN ACTIVITIES

1. *There are both benefits and challenges to moving to a new place.* Figure 2.1 lists some of the common benefits and challenges that mobile children have identified. You will notice that some experiences are both benefits *and* challenges! Establish that while there are losses involved in moving to a new place, there are also many gains.

2. *People who move have some of the same worries and concerns.* These concerns are often reflected in questions such as "Will people like me?" "Will I fit in?" "Will I make friends?" "Where is 'home?'" "Will I find my way around?" "Will I be able to learn the language?" Making new friends seems to be the greatest concern of children and adults alike. It is important for children to know that having worries is natural and that there are things they can do to help ease their worries.

3. *"Home" can mean different things to different people.* The concept of "home" is an interesting and important one to explore. It may be the place you live now, the last place you lived, the place you spend your summers, the place your family owns a home, the place your grandparents live, it may also be more than one place, or many other possibilities. Let your students tell you where "home" is for them and what it means to them. For many mobile children, "home" may become rooted in relationships with friends and family rather than a geographical place.

4. *Our special memories of people and places are a part of us.* Children not only have special memories of family and friends, but also of teachers, coaches, babysitters, and others who have been significant in their lives. They have memories of special events such as birthday parties, the school

FIGURE 2.1. Benefits and Challenges of Moving

Benefits	Challenges
Making new friends	Making new friends
Having new life experiences	Leaving family
Learning a new language	Learning a new language
Learning about different cultures	Cultural differences
Traveling to new places	Starting a new school
Making a new start	Learning your way around
Seeing new places	Different weather and climate
Meeting different kinds of people	Homesickness

play, a soccer game, and also memories of daily rituals such as waving to the crossing guard on the way to school or passing a favorite tree on the way home. Sometimes the memories of everyday things are those that are treasured most. Let your students know that it is natural to miss special people and places in our lives, and that there is a sense of loss when we leave them behind.

5. *People learn new skills from moving to a new place.* There are many cultural, interpersonal, practical, and linguistic skills that are learned from moving to a new place, even for young children. Some examples are packing their own backpacks, reading maps, negotiating airports, relating to and communicating with people of other cultures, noticing differences in behaviors and values, seeing different ways of doing things, making new friends, and learning a new language. While significant cultural differences exist between countries, differences can also exist between regions within the same country. For example, there are noticeable cultural differences between Texas and New York, Milan and Rome, or between life in the city and in the country.

6. *People who move often may develop certain characteristics.* Several characteristics of mobile children have been identified. While these characteristics are observed more often in children who have moved internationally, they may be observed in children who move domestically and frequently as well. These characteristics include the ability to adapt to new cultures, new lifestyles, new situations, and new environments; an openness to new cultures, new ways of doing things, different points of view, new experiences, and people who are different; and self-confidence and self-reliance. It is important to be aware that the continuous sense of loss experienced by individuals who move often, may cause them to withdraw

from others. These children need to be encouraged to discover ways to maintain relationships with others once they have moved away, and to continue to risk building new relationships. It is also important to realize that even though they may appear outwardly confident, mobile children often feel quite vulnerable and are afraid of making mistakes in the new culture or situation. They are concerned that they may say or do the wrong thing or wear the wrong thing, and may withdraw from activities as well as people. It is important to actively encourage their participation in the life of the school and that of the new culture or community.

Objectives: To provide students with the opportunity

- to identify the benefits and challenges in moving to a new place
- to express their worries and concerns about moving and identify ways to help ease them
- to explore what "home" is for them
- to reflect on and share special memories of the places they have lived and people they have known there
- to identify new skills they have learned as a result of their move
- to learn about some of the characteristics of people who are highly mobile

LESSON PLAN, GRADES K–2

A New Home for Tiger
by Joan Stimson

Synopsis

Tiger and his mum are moving! At first Tiger is eager to move, but when they arrive at their new home, everything is unfamiliar. Tiger longs to "go home" and when he does, he finds that the old home is now just an empty house. He begins to realize that "home" can mean different things.

Objectives

1. To provide students with the opportunity to explore the concept of "home" and discover what "home" means to them
2. To provide students with the opportunity to share their memories of a past home or homes they have lived in that have been a part of their lives

Activities Before Reading

• Have your students sit in a circle. Ask them to think about the time their parents first told them they were moving to a new home in a new neighborhood, city, state, or country. What were their reactions? How did they feel? Give each child an opportunity to share with the class. If any of your students have moved more than once, invite them to share what they remember of each move. Explain that in this story Tiger learns that he is moving to a new home.

Activities After Reading

• Discuss Tiger's feelings with your students. Ask, "How did Tiger feel about moving to the new home at first? How did he feel once he moved there?" (He was excited at first, then felt homesick, grumpy, sad, unhappy, and confused because he wasn't sure where he was.) Explain that it is natural to have many different feelings when you leave a place that was loved and familiar. You might feel both excited and sad.

• Discuss why Tiger stopped to take a last look at the old house and why he walked slowly to the new one. Ask the students what they think Tiger was thinking about. Possible responses might be "He was going to miss his old home." "He might have been remembering the good times he had there." or "He might have been worrying about what his new home would be like." Explain that we all have special memories of places we have lived.

• Children are often told they are moving but don't always understand the reasons why. Understanding the reasons for a move can make it easier to accept. This story provides an opportunity to explore the reasons families move. Ask, "Why might Tiger and his mother have moved?" Possible answers might be "It was a nicer location across the lake." "There was better hunting for food." or "They would live nearer their lion friends." Ask, "What are some of the reasons people move?" Answers could include a better quality of life, a nicer house, to experience a new place, or a parent's job transfer or job opportunity. Point out that these may be some of the reasons you and your family have moved. It is important to be aware that some children may have moved due to a natural disaster or to escape a dangerous political situation, and they may have painful memories.

• Discuss when Tiger went back to his old home, why it didn't feel right. Tiger says, "There's *no* home left in our old house. *Because it's all moved here!*" (p. 29). Discuss this with your students. Ask, "What do you think he means?" Explore the concept of "home." What is home? Is home a place? A feeling? Both? Ask, "What makes a place feel like home? What is the difference between a house and a home?" Answers may include having your things around you, people you love, what is familiar, or feeling like you belong. Ask, "What made Tiger's new home finally feel like home again?" (It took time to get used to his new surroundings, and he realized home was more than a place.) When Tiger splashed in the lake with his new friends and invited them to his house for dinner, he began making new memories in his new home. Ask your students who have moved, "What are some of the memories you've made in your new home?"

Suggested Follow-up Activities

• Have your students write, illustrate, and publish patterned books entitled *Home is . . .* Encourage them to think about the special memories they have of "home." For example, Home is . . . being with my family. Home is . . . the smell of tortillas frying in the kitchen. Home is . . . hearing my father's laughter. Home is . . . cuddling with my mom before bed. Home is . . . listening to stories in my village.

• Ask your students to bring in photographs of their old home and of their new home. Have them create a photo essay. Glue each photograph to one side of a page and have the students write or draw pictures of the special memories they have from *both* places, ones they have from their past home and ones they are creating in their current home. Establish that there are special memories to be made in the new home as well. Explain again that when Tiger splashed in the lake with his new friends and invited them to his house for dinner, he began making new memories in his new home.

• Ask the students to draw a simple blueprint of their last house. Have them draw their favorite object in each room that made the house a home, like a teddy bear in their bedroom, the rocking chair in the hallway, or a photograph of their grandparents on the wall. Have students draw a blueprint of their present home and show where their favorite objects are in this house. Talk about how those same things can move with them to help make the new house feel like home. Nonmobile children can draw a blueprint of their present home.

Transition Education Links

This story has links with objectives in Chapter 3, "The Process of Transition." Tiger's experiences can be used to learn about and discuss the different phases in the process of transition. Tiger goes through the phases in the ADAPT model (see Chapter 3), and his experiences can be related to each phase.

This story also links with objectives in Chapter 5, "Friendships and Relationships." Once Tiger realizes that his new home is "home," he begins to reach out to the other young tigers who live nearby. He went out to play with his new friends and invited them to his house for dinner. Discuss ways to make new friends and how to be a friend. Explore the ways your students can and do make new friends when they move to a new place.

LESSON PLAN, GRADES 3–5

Sarah, Plain and Tall
by Patricia MacLachlan

Synopsis

This story is set in the late nineteenth century in the midwestern part of the United States. A widowed farmer advertises in the newspaper for a wife and mother for his two children, Anna and Caleb. When Sarah arrives for a month's trial period, she is homesick for Maine, and especially misses the sea, which she dearly loves. Anna and Caleb worry that Sarah may not stay, but she grows to love the children and their father. While this is a tender story that explores the themes of love and loss, it beautifully highlights many of the experiences one has when moving to a new place.

Objectives

1. To provide students with the opportunity to share their special memories of places they have lived, what they miss, and how they keep those memories alive
2. To provide students with the opportunity to explore the benefits and challenges they find in moving to a new place
3. To provide students with the opportunity to express their worries and concerns associated with moving and find ways to ease them
4. To provide students with the opportunity to identify the skills they have learned as a result of their move

Activities Before Reading

• Ask the students to think about a time when they moved to a new place or visited a place that was different from what they had experienced before. Have them consider some of the things they had to adjust to and share their experiences with the class. These may include things such as climate, weather, geography, food, language, customs, transportation, population, leaving family and friends, and a new school. Explain that in *Sarah, Plain and Tall* Sarah has many adjustments to make in her life as well.

Activities After Reading

• Discuss the adjustments Sarah had to make in moving from Maine to the prairie. (These include being away from her family, different surroundings, living far from town, and meeting new people.)

• In the story Sarah tells Matthew, "There is always things to miss, no matter where you are" (p. 43). Invite the children to respond to this idea. Do they agree or disagree? They are likely to share things they miss in their lives. Explain that our memories are a part of us, and that it is natural to miss special people and places we have left behind and to feel a sense of loss. Our memories may include friends, family, sights, smells, possessions, feelings, experiences, pets, and more. Sarah had special memories of her life in Maine. Discuss these with the class. What were they? How did she keep her memories alive? Chart responses (see Figure 2.2 for sample responses).

Ask your students, "What are some of your own special memories? How do you keep the memories of people, places, and things you love alive?" Have them complete a similar chart, also including ways they *could* keep their memories alive (see Figure 2.3 for a sample chart). Have the children share their charts with a partner and see if they can offer each other suggestions as well. Ask each child to choose one or two memories to share with the entire class.

• Maggie brought Sarah plants and told her, "You must have a garden. Wherever you are" (p. 41). Are there any traditions you and your family have when you move to a new place?

FIGURE 2.2. Sarah's Memories

Sarah's memories	Ways she kept her memories alive
The sea	Brought a collection of shells with her Kept them on the windowsill Brought a conch shell so she could hear the sea Brought colored pencils to draw pictures of the sea Talked about it
The seals, whales, and sea birds	Told Anna, Caleb, and Jacob about them
Her brother, William	Wrote letters and sent pictures to him Talked about him
Her aunts	Named the sheep after them
Sliding in the sand dunes as a child	Shared her memories Made a hay dune

FIGURE 2.3. Memories

My memories	Ways I keep my memories alive	Ways I could keep my memories alive

• Sarah brought her treasured shells to the prairie and even brought them to the barn during the storm. Are there "treasured objects" you always bring with you when you move? Do you keep them in a special place? These could be photographs, stuffed animals, books, letters, mementos, or a friendship bracelet. Explain that our "treasured objects" can comfort us during times of change and help us stay connected to our past. Have nonmobile students share their treasured objects as well and what they *would* bring with them if they moved.

• Using a Venn diagram, have the students compare the characteristics of life in Maine to life on the prairie (see Figure 2.4). From the information in the diagram, chart the benefits and challenges Sarah experienced (see Figure 2.5). Once you have modeled this with the class, ask the students to complete their own Venn diagrams comparing the place they live now to the last place they lived. Have them list the benefits and challenges they have experienced, and then share the diagram and chart with a partner. Ask each student to choose a benefit and challenge to share with the class and to identify a new skill they have learned as a result of their move. Nonmobile students can complete this activity comparing their home to that of another family member, a place they have visited, or a regular vacation destination. They could also list the benefits and challenges of moving versus staying.

• Point out that there are often language differences even if you live in the same country. Just like with *ayuh* and *yes*, there are different expressions in different regions. Some others might include *bag* and *sack*, *pop* and *soda*. Your students will probably be able to add to the list. With international students, you can all learn the different ways to say *hello* and *goodbye* in the languages spoken by children in your classroom.

FIGURE 2.4. Venn Diagram Comparing Maine to the Prairie

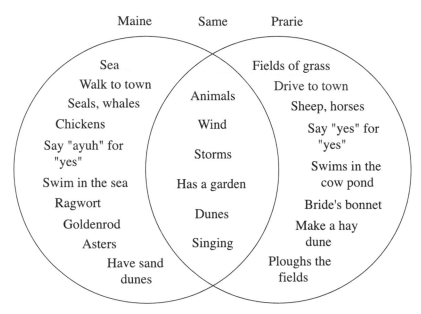

Maine   Same   Prarie

Maine	Same	Prarie
Sea	Animals	Fields of grass
Walk to town	Wind	Drive to town
Seals, whales	Storms	Sheep, horses
Chickens	Has a garden	Say "yes" for "yes"
Say "ayuh" for "yes"	Dunes	Swims in the cow pond
Swim in the sea	Singing	Bride's bonnet
Ragwort		Make a hay dune
Goldenrod		Ploughs the fields
Asters		
Have sand dunes		

• Have your students sit in a circle. Explain that people usually have worries and concerns about moving to a new place even if they are excited about the move. With your students, list some of the worries people might have and chart them. Ask, "What do you think were some of the worries Sarah had in moving to the prairie?" Ideas might include leaving her family, wondering if she would still have her independence living so far from town, if she could bring her cat, if she would be lonely, if she would make new friends, if she could bear being away from the sea, and if she would like the Witting family and if they would like her.

FIGURE 2.5. Benefits and Challenges of Moving to the Prairie

Benefits	Challenges
Learned new skills, such as riding a horse, driving a wagon, and ploughing the fields	Being away from her family
	Missing her brother and aunts
	Feeling lonely
Had new experiences	Giving up the sea that she loved
Made a new friend in Maggie	Living far from town
Found a new family to love	

Ask, "What were some of the worries you had when you moved or would have if you were to move?" Go around the circle and give each child a chance to share.

Then ask, "What things did Sarah do to ease her worries?" (Some strategies were that she found out about the new place, asked questions, learned new skills to help her, and found a way to do the things she enjoyed in the new place, like swimming in the cow pond instead of the sea and sliding on a hay dune instead of a sand dune.)

Also ask, "What are some of the things you could do to ease your worries if you were moving to a new place?" Ideas could include finding out about the new place, asking questions, talking to friends and family, keeping a journal, and learning some words in the new language. Again, give each child in the circle a chance to share a response.

• Sarah says, "I will always miss my old home, but the truth of it is, I would miss you more" (p. 57). Explore the concept of "home." Together with your students pose questions to be discussed in a sharing circle, for example, "What is 'home?'" "Do you always miss your old home?" "What makes a place 'home?'" "Is 'home' always a place?" "Can more than one place be 'home?'" Establish that "home" means different things to different people.

Suggested Follow-up Activities

• "I used to . . . but now" poems are an excellent way for children to express the changes in their lives. Share this sample poem, given below, with your students. Point out the way the poem reflects Sarah's new experiences and new skills as well as her memories. Then have the children write their own "I used to . . . but now" poems that reflect their moves to different cities, states, or countries. These poems can be compiled in a class book or included in a poetry anthology.

I used to . . . but now

I used to live near the sea in Maine
But now my home is on the prairie.
I used to rest my eyes on white-capped waves
But now I see rolling fields for miles around.
I used to walk to town past shingled houses
But now I drive a wagon through fields of gold.
I used to splash about in the salty sea
But now I gaze up at the sky as I float in the cow pond.
I used to stroke seals and watch the whales in the distance
But now I run with the lambs and feel their coarse wool.

I used to live with my brother and visit my aunts
But now I have a new family to love as well.

- Have students respond to what "home" means to them. Encourage them to write poems, narratives, or songs, or create art projects that reflect their idea of "home." Brainstorm other ideas together.
- Have your students compile a *Tips for Moving* class book based on their ideas for how to ease the worry of moving to a new place.

Transition Education Links

This story has links with objectives in Chapter 3, "The Process of Transition." Discuss what happens to the person who is not moving but is staying behind like Sarah's brother, William. What concerns do people have when they do not move, but a good friend or family member moves away? Have your students write an imaginary letter from William to Sarah sharing his concerns and feelings now that she has left. If any of your students have been left behind, encourage them to write to the person who has moved expressing their feelings.

This story also has links with objectives in Chapter 5, "Friendships and Relationships." Having moved herself, Maggie senses that Sarah is homesick and reaches out to her in friendship. With your students, explore ways that they could reach out to others who are new to a place and most likely missing their old home.

Sarah writes to her brother and also sends him pictures of the new people and places in her life on the prairie. In this way she lets him know about her new life. Explore ways your students can keep in touch with the people in their lives in meaningful ways and let them know about their new experiences.

LESSON PLAN, GRADES K–5

Painted Words and Spoken Memories
by Aliki

Synopsis

This book has been designed in two parts. The first part of this book is entitled *Painted Words*. When Marianthe (Mari) and her family move from Greece to America, she is nervous about going to her new school because she doesn't speak any English. While her teacher is nice and most of the other children accept her, Marianthe feels overwhelmed with the new sights and the sounds of the new language. Her mother encourages her to watch and listen, and use her body language to communicate with her new classmates, but it isn't always that easy. Fortunately, her teacher encourages her to paint pictures to express herself, and she paints pictures of her family and her old home. Through her paintings she is able to communicate and express her feelings about being new in a new country. The second part of the book, *Spoken Memories*, picks up when Marianthe has learned enough English to share during Life-Story time and tell her story of coming to America. It is through this second sharing, the spoken part, that her classmates learn more about her life back in her former home, and why her family moved to America. The two stories are a perfect complement to each other.

Objectives

1. To provide students with the opportunity to explore the benefits and challenges in moving to a new place, particularly in moving to a new country
2. To provide students with the opportunity to express their worries and concerns associated with moving and find ways to ease them
3. To provide students with the opportunity to share sensory memories of places they have left behind
4. To provide students with the opportunity to identify new skills they have learned as a result of their move

Activities Before Reading

• Explain to the students that this book has been designed in a unique format, telling two stories of the same event, a young girl's move from Greece to America. The first part of the book is told mainly through the young girl's painted artwork, and the second part is told through her spoken words. Ask students to listen carefully to both parts and decide which part they enjoyed the most, or if both parts were necessary to complement each other in providing the full story.

• Ask students to think of a time when they were the new person at school and what their concerns were. Then tell them to listen while you read the story of Marianthe's move to America.

Activities After Reading

• After reading the book aloud, ask your students which part of the book they liked the most, the *Painted Words* or the *Spoken Memories*. Then ask if the book was better with both parts together. Explain that people usually have different preferences for how they express themselves, and that you are going to give the students an opportunity later to choose their preferred mode of expression.

• Have the students generate a list of worries that Marianthe had about moving to America and starting over at a new school. (She wouldn't know anyone, she wouldn't understand what they were saying, and they wouldn't understand her.) Ask students to reflect on a time when they had to move and were the "new kid at school." Ask them to think about their worries. Hand out strips of paper and tell students to choose their top three worries about going to a new school, possibly for some in a new country. Ask them to write one worry per strip. After they have written these worries down, get out a large paper bag and tell students to drop their worry strips in the "worry bag." Then pull out strips one by one and read each worry aloud, without identifying whose worry it was. Have students brainstorm ways to help solve this worry. An example of a worry might be "I was worried that no one would like me." A brainstormed solution might be "Be sure to smile, so people know you are a friendly person." Another worry might be "I was worried that I didn't speak the language." The solution might be "Listen to your classmates speak and try to say some words." After all the worry strips have been read, students should see a pattern of similarities. Talk about how everyone usually has worries when they are going to move, even if they are excited about it, and these worries are often similar regardless of age. Remind them of the brainstormed possibilities for solutions. Consider charting their suggestions or compiling them in a class book *Useful Tips for Moving*.

• Now ask students to think back to a particular move that they made. Using their five senses, ask students to think vividly about the place they moved from. Have them write down the sights, sounds, and smells (pleasant and unpleasant) that they remember from their former house or apartment. Ask them to pair up with a partner and describe those sights, sounds, and smells. Then ask them to describe emotions about their home, what made it so special or not so special—it is important to note that some children may be leaving a place with unhappy memories. These emotions are usually nothing tangible like the five senses, but will deal with feelings. Then draw a large *H* on the front board. List their sensory words about their house on the left of the *H*, and their emotional words about their home on the right of the *H*. Then ask, "What is the special ingredient that bonds a house and home together?" Most of them will say "family." Then put the bonding word on the crossbar of the *H* so that they can see what helps them bridge from a building to a sense of belonging. The "family" is also the key ingredient that will help them bridge from their former home to their new one, even if it is in a new country.

• Give your students an opportunity to draw or paint or write about a vivid memory from a place where they have lived before. Display the finished products on two walls in your classroom: a Spoken Memories Wall and a Painted Words Wall. Have students present aloud the written pieces and consider making a class tape or videotape of *Our Special Memories*.

• There are many reasons people move to another city, state, or coun try. Why did Mari's family decide to move? (Her parents wanted a better life for their children following the war.) Discuss other reasons families might move. The children may give reasons such a parent's job or to be closer to family. Some children, particularly immigrant and refugee children, may have moved due to civil unrest, political upheaval, or natural disasters. Be aware that they may have painful memories and powerful feelings.

• Mari faced many challenges when her family decided to move to America. What was the first challenge she faced without even leaving the country? (It was difficult being apart from her father.) How did Mari keep in touch with him? (She sent letters and drew pictures of what they were doing in the village.) Point out that many families often have to live apart for a period of time at some point during a move, particularly in a move to another country. This can be very difficult for everyone. Discuss how families can stay close during that time.

• Discuss the challenges Mari faced when she arrived in America. (They include learning a new language, adjusting to a new school, adjusting to a new culture, being away from her family in Greece and her close neighbors, and making new friends.) Discuss the benefits Mari experienced. (They include a formal education, learning another language, making new friends, and experiencing a new country.) Have your students share the benefits and challenges they experienced when they moved. Discuss the differences and similarities of moving to a different country or to a new place within your own country. Chart and compare these with your students. Consider pairing nonmobile and mobile students to discuss the benefits of moving versus staying behind.

• Mari learns many new skills from her move to America. What are they? The students are likely to say that she made new friends and learned to speak another language. Point out that she also learns some very important skills for adjusting to a new culture. Mari's mother tells her to look, listen, and learn, and that a body can talk, eyes speak many words, and a smile is a smile in any language. What do you think she means? Why is this useful advice? Explain that there may be differences in body language between cultures, but a smile of friendship or kindness is universal. Ask your students for their ideas for adjusting to a new place and a new cul-

ture. Have your students list the new skills they have learned as a result of
their move and share them with the class.

Suggested Follow-up Activities

• Mr. Petrie says there is more than one way to tell a story. Mari tells
her story through painting and speaking. Explain that there are many different ways we can express ourselves. Ask your students to choose a way to
tell their life story. Brainstorm ideas together. Ideas could include writing
a skit, composing a song, writing their memoirs, making a collage journal,
or writing a poem. Encourage students to include some of their special
memories.

• Mari experiences the kindness of children who reach out to her
and make an effort to communicate with her by using body language.
She also experiences the unkind actions of others, like Patrick, who make
fun of her. This is an excellent opportunity to develop empathy with your
students. Ask, "Why do you think Patrick teased Mari?" "How did Mari
feel?" Mari's mother tells her that there will always be those who hurt
and tease out of ignorance. Discuss the meaning of ignorance, explaining that it is a lack of knowledge or awareness. Discuss the issues that
were probably raised when the children talked about Mari's painting and
hurt feelings in their class meeting. Explore ways we can all reach out to
those who are new and help them feel included, especially if they do not
speak the same language.

Transition Education Links

This story has links with objectives in Chapter 3, "The Process of Transition" as it provides a framework from which to teach cross-cultural skills.
Look, listen, and learn is sound advice for approaching the process of transition. Explore other effective strategies that can be used to adapt to a new
culture. (See Appendix E.)

It also links with objectives in Chapter 4, "Personal and Cultural Identity." When Mari shares her life story, she shares many of her family and
cultural traditions from her life in Greece. Provide an opportunity for your
students to share their family and cultural traditions, which may be a blend
of several cultures. For internationally mobile children and their families,
their cultural traditions may be influenced by the many places they have
lived and may continue to change to incorporate their different experiences.

It links well with objectives in Chapter 5, "Friendships and Relationships." It provides an opportunity for children to gain an understanding
of what it is like to be new in a different country and to learn a new lan-

guage. Explore additional ways to reach out and welcome those who are new to the class, school, and community.

This story also links with objectives in Chapter 6, "Problem-Solving Skills." Mari and her mother say good-bye to the people and the village they love and to all the things they knew—the trees, the rocks, the birds— before they leave for America. Give your students the opportunity to share the people, places, and things they said good-bye to or would have liked to have said good-bye to before they moved. Discuss the importance of saying good-bye and explore how to say good-bye in meaningful ways.

LESSON PLAN, GRADES K–5

Gila Monsters Meet You at the Airport
by Marjorie Weinman Sharmat

Synopsis

While written in a humorous way, this story explores the fears children have about moving to a new place. It begins in New York City with a young boy whose family is moving out West. He has many worries and misconceptions about what life will be like there, and his best friend, Seymour, has even told him that Gila monsters meet you at the airport! When the boy arrives at the airport out West, he meets another boy who is moving East who has his own misconceptions about life in New York City. The boy soon discovers the West is not as bad as he had imagined after all.

Objectives

1. To provide students with the opportunity to talk about their fears of moving to a new place and find ways to address them
2. To provide students with the opportunity to discover some of the characteristics of people who move

Activities Before Reading

• Ask your students to share the things they were concerned about when they had to move to a new home. Include your nonmobile students by asking them what they *would* be concerned about. Chart the responses. Ask them why situations that are new are sometimes scary. Together make a list of the things that might be different in a new home, school, neighborhood, or country. The list is likely to include food, transportation, climate, buildings and architecture, language or languages spoken, ways of doing things, and ways things look and sound. Introduce the story by asking your students to predict what the story might be about from the title and cover. Establish that in this story a young boy has many worries when he has to move to a new place.

Activities After Reading

• Make a list with your students of the things the boy in the story was worried about when he found out that he and his parents were moving out West. Including what his best friend tells him, there are 10 worries or misconceptions he has about the West:

1. Out West nobody plays baseball because they're too busy chasing buffaloes.
2. There are cactuses everywhere you look.
3. It takes 15 minutes just to say hello because people talk so slowly.
4. He'll look silly all the time because he'll have to wear chaps, spurs, a bandanna, and a hat so big that nobody will be able to find him underneath.
5. He'll have to ride a horse to school, and he doesn't know how.
6. Everybody grows up to be a sheriff.
7. He probably won't have any friends, but if he does they'll be named Tex or Slim.
8. He'll have to eat chili and beans for breakfast, lunch, and dinner.
9. The desert is so hot you can collapse, and then buzzards circle overhead and no one rescues you.
10. Gila monsters meet you at the airport.

After making the list, ask the students to see if they can figure out categories that some of the items would fit into. For example, when the boy worries that all they'll have to eat is chili and beans, that category might be "food." Then initiate a conversation with your students about the categories themselves. Help them to see that many of our fears about the unknown revolve around our basic needs of food, clothing, and shelter, and our social needs of safety and acceptance. Explain that when we move, we often worry about everyday things like what kinds of food we will have to eat, where we will live, and how we'll get around. We also worry about making friends and fitting in, and being embarrassed if we say or do the wrong thing. Compare this list with the class list of the students' own worries and look for similar categories.

• Discuss ways the boy in the story could have eased his fears about moving out West. Suggestions may include talking with his parents or teacher about his fears, asking them questions about the West, and asking them to help him find information about the West from books and magazines or on the Internet. Suggest that these are strategies your students can also use when they are worried about an upcoming move or other change in their lives. Ask your students to share other effective strategies they have used to ease their fears when they have moved in the past or faced a new situation.

• This story provides an excellent opportunity to explore the nature of misconceptions and stereotypes, and the ways they are formed. Explain to your students that we often have an idea about people and places from what we hear, read, or see on television or in the movies. While there may be some truth to the information we get this way, it is inaccurate to generalize and judge all people and places in a particular way. Point out that many of the boy's worries were actually misconceptions or stereotypes of the West. Help your students to see the importance of reserving judgment until they learn about new people and places. Discuss and role-play situations where stereotyping might occur in your community, and effective and safe ways to deal with it.

• The boy's fears about the West were eased once he began to observe what life was really like there. Have your students work with a partner to find examples of information in both the text and illustrations that counter his misconceptions, although they may contain some truth. These include the following: He sees clouds in the sky, but no buzzards from the airplane window; there may be Gila monsters, but they don't meet you at the airport; it's warm, but there's a breeze; there aren't any buffalo stampedes; there is a restaurant just like the one back East; he sees kids playing baseball; when he sees kids riding bikes by his house, one kid has a baseball cap and the other a cowboy hat, but neither kid is wearing chaps, spurs, and a bandanna; there are horses, but he won't have to ride to school; and there are some cactuses, but not everywhere.

• Give your students a large piece of paper and have them fold it in fourths. In the top two squares, ask them to choose a part of the story that appeals to them and illustrate the misconception about the West on the left side and the reality of that situation on the right. For example, they may illustrate the Gila monsters meeting the plane on one side and ordinary people meeting the plane on the other. In the bottom two squares, ask them to choose a misconception they had about moving to the place they live now and the reality of the situation. Children who haven't moved can draw about a place they visited or learned about where something was different than they expected. Have your students share their drawings with the class.

• Explain to your students that we can learn some positive strategies from the boy in the story about how to approach moving to a new place. Despite his fears, he demonstrates certain characteristics that help him adjust to his new location. See if your students can infer some of these characteristics from the story. For example, he is observant and learns about his new surroundings; he is interested in what it is like out West; he is interested in finding things he likes to do; he is open to new experiences and appreciates what the new place has to offer like riding horses; and he seems open to making new friends with the kids on the bikes. Some of the beneficial characteristics of people who move are the ability to adapt to new cultures, new lifestyles, and new situations, and an openness to new experiences and new ways of doing things. On the last page of the story, the boy has traded his baseball cap for a cowboy hat. He is already beginning to see himself as a Westerner. While it takes time to adjust to a new place, the boy seems open to the new experience. Recognize, however, that not *all* people are open to new experiences at first.

Suggested Follow-up Activities

• Initiate a discussion about the boy he met at the airport who was moving to the East. Why would that boy have so many strange misconceptions about New York City? Why is it that all people who move worry about what their new life will be like? Have the students write postcards between the two boys. What would they tell each other about their new home? This can be done as a shared writing activity for younger children. Alternatively, have students write a letter from the boy to his old friend Seymour telling him what life is really like out West.
• Children can write songs, poems, or create comic strips or skits depicting the imagined fears they have had about moving.

Transition Education Links

The story has links with Chapter 3, "The Process of Transition." It can be used to explain the different stages people go through when moving to a new place. Using the ADAPT model explained in Chapter 3, initiate a discussion inviting your students to share their experiences of these stages. Ask them how the boy in the story fits in the different stages. The story begins with him in the "Don't want to go, or do I?" stage (Leaving Stage). When he is in the airplane on the way out West, he is in the "Anything is possible!" stage (Transition Stage), where so much is unknown. He isn't even sure where "home" is on the map. Once he arrives, he is beginning to move into the "Perhaps this isn't so bad" stage (Entering Stage). Although it takes time to reach this stage, we can tell by the boy's attitude that he is open to the new experience and willing to become part of the new community.

You can use this story to further develop effective strategies to manage transition. The boy's fears were eased once he began to experience the West. Brainstorm ways we can approach a new situation we are worried about, particularly a move to a new place. Some suggestions might be to take risks; be open-minded, curious, and patient; have a sense of humor; be willing to make mistakes; and be willing to laugh at ourselves. Suggest that while it is natural to be a little scared when moving to a new place, you should try to keep your fears at bay and contain your imagination and don't let it run wild, because you really don't know what a place is like until you get there. Sometimes you just have to wait until you arrive to know what a place is really like.

This story also provides an opportunity to discuss cultural adaptation and culture shock with your students. When the boy first arrives out West he wants to ask his parents for a horse, trades his baseball cap for a cowboy hat, and sees himself as a Westerner. Explain that this is typical of the honeymoon period when everything in the new place is novel and exciting. It is likely that the boy will eventually experience some degree of culture shock as he will have to adapt to many things out West that are different from things in New York, and there will be things he will miss. They might include the weather, the tall buildings of the city, his friend Seymour, or living in a house versus an apartment. Have your students share some of the things that they had to adapt to and that were confusing for them when they moved to their current home.

LESSON PLAN, GRADE 5

Bloomability
by Sharon Creech

Synopsis

Dinnie knows about change! She and her family constantly move from state to state as her father seeks out yet another new job opportunity. But when her Aunt Sandy and Uncle Max arrange for her to attend an international school in Lugano, Switzerland, where her uncle has been appointed the new headmaster, Dinnie is not sure this is for her. This story sensitively and authentically captures the thoughts, feelings, and experiences children have when they move internationally. As Dinnie learns to adapt to a new country and culture, as well as a new home, and makes new friends

(Guthrie, Lila), she discovers the many "bloomabilities" life has to offer. This book addresses many of the transition issues children experience when they move to another country and has excellent links with each chapter.

Objectives

1. To provide students with the opportunity to share their experiences of moving to a new place and to identify the benefits and challenges they found
2. To provide students with the opportunity to express their worries and concerns about moving and find ways to ease them
3. To provide students with the opportunity to explore the concept of "home" and discover what home means to them
4. To provide students with the opportunity to identify the new skills they have learned as a result of their move
5. To provide students with the opportunity to learn about some of the characteristics of people who are mobile

Activities Before Reading

• Ask your students to reflect on their move to the place they are living now. Have them write a piece entitled, *The Big Move*, beginning with when they first heard the news that they were moving and describing how they adapted to the new place they live now, including their thoughts and feelings about the experience. Ask your students who have not moved to speculate on how they would react if they were moving abroad. How would they feel? What worries and concerns would they have? Provide an opportunity for your students to share their pieces if they choose. Make sure that you respond to them in writing as they will probably contain some very personal and significant feelings.

• Explain that this is a story about a girl named Dinnie, who has moved to another country. Whether you have moved or not, you will gain a greater understanding about the experiences people have when they move, particularly abroad.

• Discuss the word *bloomability* and ask your students what they think it means. After reading, ask the students to consider why the author chose this word as the title of the book. Is it fitting?

Activities After Reading

• At the end of the story, Dinnie feels very much at home in Switzerland and no longer like a stranger. She thinks of herself as a snail carting her home and family along with her on her back. She realizes she can bring her memories of Switzerland and the people she knew there with her when she leaves. Dinnie carries her sense of "home" with her. Explain to your students that people often develop strong ties to places they have lived and people they have known there, and these people and places become a part of them in some way. Explore what "home" means to each of them.

• Based on the map in the front of the book showing Dinnie's "second life," have your students create a pictorial map reflecting their own personal history. Have them begin with the place they live now. Ask them to then include the other places they have lived and the special places that made each place "home" such as their school, house, friend's house, a favorite park, the beach, and so on.

• One of Dinnie's worries was that her family back home would forget about her. She missed them and wrote letters to them. Dinnie corresponded regularly with her two favorite aunts who sent postcards letting her know what was going on in their lives as well as asking about hers. In this way they were able to stay close. Discuss the worries and concerns your students had or have about moving. A common concern is leaving friends and family behind. Some children may not be able to contact friends and family due to the political situation they left behind. Discuss ways to manage the worry when you are out of touch with family and friends.

Have your students design a series of postcards of special scenes in the place they live now. This could include their house, places of cultural interest, friends, or their favorite places to visit or just hang out. They can draw the pictures or scan drawings or photographs into the computer and print them to make cards. Have them send the cards to friends and family to keep in touch and let them know about their life in the place they now live.

• Dinnie learns to speak some Italian, ski, find her way around in a foreign country, and make new friends. Have your students discuss the new skills they have learned as a result of their move or moves.

• Dinnie brings her "box of things" with her when she moves. It contains her fishing rod, her book of dreams, and her list of all the places she has lived, among other things. Ask, "What treasured objects do you bring with you or would you bring when you move?" "What activities do you enjoy and how have you found a way to do them living here?"

• Have your students work with a partner to examine the text more closely to find passages that contain an insight into, or message about, moving or living in another country that they think is valuable. Ask each pair to share these with the class. Encourage your class to think of their own suggestions for approaching a move to another place or country, and publish an advice guide for moving that can be given to new students who arrive in your school.

Suggested Follow-up Activities

Writing and reflection

• Like Guthrie, have your students write a graduation speech highlighting the benefits they see in the experience of living abroad or in a new place.

• Guthrie reads the poem "The Road Not Taken" by Robert Frost as part of his graduation speech. Read and discuss this poem with your students. Ask, "What does making a choice mean?" While they probably had no choice in moving, they do have a choice as to how they respond to the move. Ask, "What choices have you made in moving here? Have you decided to become part of the life of the school and your new community?" Point out that the road less traveled is often the more interesting one. Discuss this. Have your students look for other poems that relate to the experience of moving to another place. Encourage your students to write their own poetry that relates to the experience of transition, and compile a class anthology of poetry.

• There is a lovely description of spring in Lugano at the beginning of Chapter 42. Use this as an example of descriptive writing and have your students write a descriptive piece that evokes a sense of place from their last home or place where they have special memories.

• Dinnie has the summer to decide what to do the following year. Ask your students what they think Dinnie decided to do: Did she stay in the United States or return to Switzerland? Why? Have them write a letter from Dinnie to Aunt Sandy and Uncle Max, revealing her decision and her thoughts behind it.

• At first Dinnie did not see the benefit of moving to Switzerland, although she eventually came to appreciate the new experiences she had. Ask your students to write a letter from Dinnie to her aunt and uncle thanking them for the opportunities she had in her year abroad. Consider asking your students to write a thank-you note to their parents showing their appreciation for the opportunities they have been given as a result of living abroad or in the new location.

Discussion and reflection

• In the story, the students participate in "thinking" discussions in their English class. Ask your students to come up with a list of questions they would like to discuss that relate to moving, and address them in a "thinking" or philosophy circle.

- Have your students create mobiles that reflect their "bloomabilities" —the experiences, both benefits and challenges, that have helped them grow and flourish in their new location.

- Discuss the idea that people who move, particularly those who move often, sometimes develop certain characteristics. These characteristics may be part of their personality or develop from their life experiences of moving. Some people may be like Gutlirle and approach a move to a new place with curiosity and enthusiasm. Other people may be more like Lila and feel frustrated when things are different from what they know. Some people reach out to others and make friends easily, while others are reluctant to get close to people because they may lose them again when they or the other people move. Ask, "Are there any characteristics you have noticed about yourself when you moved to a new place or entered a new situation?"

Transition Education Links

This story has many links with Chapter 3, "The Process of Transition." After arriving in Lugano, Dinnie thinks, "Later I would be able to look at this view and to see it and appreciate it, and it would affect me profoundly. But on that first day, I could only see what wasn't there, my family" (p. 24). Have students share what it was like for them when they first arrived in the place they live now. Were there certain things they were missing? What were they?

Teach your students about the different stages in the transition process. Explain each of the stages and together with your students, relate them to Dinnie's experiences in the book. For example, when Dinnie arrives and makes the statement above, she is in the "Anything is possible!" stage (Transition Stage). Have your students who have moved identify which stage of the process they see themselves in now. Ask them to complete a chart of the different stages of the process of transition, describing their thoughts, feelings, and experiences in each stage.

Dinnie and her aunt respond differently to the experience of moving. Her aunt loves Switzerland, while it takes Dinnie time to adapt to her new home. Ask, "How did you respond when you moved? Was it the same or different from the response of other members in your family?"

Lila goes through a "honeymoon" period when she first arrives in Switzerland and thinks everything is wonderful. She then experiences culture shock and becomes critical, demanding, and sometimes insensitive to other cultures. Ask, "Why do you think Lila had such a difficult time adjusting in her move to Switzerland? What advice would you give to her?"

Some suggestions might be to be open to new experiences, give the new place a chance, observe differences without making judgments, or talk with teachers or the headmaster if she is upset. Acknowledge that there were family problems that contributed to the difficult time Lila was having, and that the stresses of moving can cause problems within a family. Be sensitive to the fact that some of your students may have similar experiences at home. It is not unusual for a move to occur as a result of a parent's separation, divorce, or remarriage. A move can also occur due to political upheaval, civil unrest, or natural disasters.

Guthrie tells Dinnie a story about two prisoners: When they looked out of the small window in their cell, one prisoner saw dirt and the other saw sky. Ask your students what they think the message is in this story? A possible answer might be that we experience what we see. How does this relate to the experience of moving?

Dinnie describes some of her experiences learning Italian. While she is beginning to recognize words and phrases, it is often confusing and frustrating. Learning a new language is part of adapting to a new country and culture. Discuss suggestions your students have for ways to approach learning a new language. Include things they can do that would help them learn a new language as well as ways they can help someone who is learning their language.

This story also has links with Chapter 4, "Personal and Cultural Identity." Dinnie finds that the other students at her international school come from and/or have lived in many different countries. She learns that it is not easy to tell someone's nationality from his or her appearance. Point out that our cultural backgrounds are rich and varied, and many people are from multicultural families and have several cultural influences in their lives. Provide opportunities for your students to share their cultural backgrounds and learn about the cultural backgrounds of their classmates.

Dinnie begins to explore her Italian roots while living in Lugano. Consider having your students create a modified family history project. Have them interview family members to learn more about their cultural heritage, create a family tree, and present their findings, including family photographs and artifacts.

This story also has links with Chapter 5, "Friendships and Relationships." Dinnie thinks about her friends and the other children at the international school. She observes that for all their differences in nationality, language, culture, and personality, they were more alike than different. Discuss this idea with your students. In what ways are people alike regardless of their differences?

Dinnie accepts people as they are and recognizes that making new friends takes time. These are positive approaches to making new friends.

Provide an opportunity for your students to share other strategies that have helped them develop new relationships.

There are also links with objectives in Chapter 6, "Problem-Solving Skills." Dinnie says good-bye to the special places she frequented in Montagnola and Lugano. She also includes photographs of her friends and mementos of trips and events in her special box. Have your students devise a moving plan that includes the people and places they would say good-bye to before they moved away.

Due to family circumstances, Lila has to leave Lugano suddenly. Explain that this is difficult for both the person who leaves and the people left behind. Brainstorm ways to say good-bye when there is little or no time to do so. This may include sharing thoughts in a letter to the person after he or she has moved. This may be a useful activity for immigrant, refugee, or other children who had to leave at short notice.

There are also links with objectives in Chapter 7, "Moving Back." Dinnie wonders what she will find when she returns home to Bybanks, Kentucky. How will it look, smell, and be to see her family again? Invite your students who are moving back to a former home to share their expectations and concerns. Discuss ways to reestablish relationships with people when you have been away. Some suggestions may be to show an interest in other people's lives and realize that it often takes time to regain the level of closeness you once had. If you have students who are moving back home or have recently done so, ask them what things they wondered about? Were there ways they could get information to answer questions they had?

Dinnie realizes that returning to Bybanks will be "an opportunity. A new life" (p. 272). This attitude reflects an openness she has developed and what she has learned about change and moving; that "bloomabilities" are possible anywhere. Ask, "What attitudes have you developed from your experiences living abroad or in a different place?"

CROSS-CURRICULAR CONNECTIONS

Creative and Performing Arts

Have students look at paintings and drawings of people, places, and things that evoke a strong feeling. Discuss how the artist conveys this to the viewer. Have students bring in photographs, letters, artifacts, and so on that evoke special memories. Ask them to draw or paint a picture that captures a special memory for them. Consider different media such as colored pencils, pastels, watercolors, and so on. Discuss techniques and use of color and shading to convey the feeling of the piece.

Discuss different ways human beings express themselves. Explore ways of expression that involve performance. Have students express their feelings and concerns about moving through music (different instruments can be used to convey different feelings), dance, or drama (e.g., skits or a dramatic reading of a poem about moving).

Social Studies

Provide opportunities for your students to share their backgrounds and special memories through social studies topics studied such as Families, All About Me, and Countries and Cultures. Like Mari in *Painted Words and Spoken Memories*, they can tell their life story. They can create time lines of significant events in their lives, create collage journals, or write a short play.

Map skills can be included as students create maps to represent their life journey and moves from place to place. They can create maps of their new neighborhood or school to learn more about their new surroundings.

You can tie in a personal look at the benefits and challenges of moving as part of a study of immigration or migration.

Science

As part of a study of the brain and nervous system, learn about how memories are formed. Explain that the hippocampus is one part of our brain that creates memories. Our sense of smell has a strong and direct connection to the hippocampus, so therefore smells often trigger memories. Bring in several items for your students to smell and have them record the memories these smells evoke. Share with a partner. Are there particular smells from their past homes that bring back certain memories?

Differences in climate can be a challenge in adjusting to a new place. Compare climates and weather patterns in the different places your students have lived as part of a study of weather.

Math

Have students create graphs of the number of times classmates have moved or the different countries in which they have lived.

Chapter 3

The Process of Transition

Whenever we experience transition in our lives there is a process we go through marked by different stages. There are several models that describe the process of transition involved in moving. We particularly like the one developed by David Pollock, Director of Interaction, Inc., and a leading authority in the field of transition and international mobility. While Pollock & Van Reken (1999) developed this model with internationally mobile students in mind, it is a model that can be applied to domestic mobility as well. This model is extremely useful in helping children and adults make sense of their experiences and understand the changes they are going through when they move.

Depending on the degree of mobility in your particular community, children may be moving to or from your school at any point throughout the school year. It is therefore important for you to learn about the transition stages and the experiences associated with them.

THE TRANSITION EXPERIENCE

Pollock has identified five stages that individuals move through when they experience the transitions involved in moving to a new place. These are *involvement, leaving, transition, entering*, and *reinvolvement*; and there are different feelings and common experiences associated with each stage.

• *Involvement Stage*. In the involvement stage we feel at home in the place we are living. We feel settled and have a sense of belonging and a sense of place in our community. This familiarity provides a level of comfort and sense of security in our lives.

• *Leaving Stage*. Once we learn we will be moving, we enter the leaving stage. In this stage life begins to change as we begin to focus on the future. We may begin to distance ourselves from personal relationships and responsibilities, and others may withdraw from us as well. It is important, however, to make sure that we do not disengage from relationships too soon and that this tendency is addressed with children. It is not unusual to see children withdraw prematurely or create conflicts with their friends during this stage because they think it is easier to leave someone with whom they are angry. There are many mixed emotions during this time, and we may not be sure if we want to go or stay. We are often excited and anxious at the same time, as friends and family plan celebrations and farewells to mark our leaving and we anticipate the future. We may also feel sad and lonely as plans are made for events we will not be there to attend, and we may feel angry over the lack of control we had in the decision to move.

• *Transition Stage.* The transition stage begins when we actually leave the place where we are living. It is a time of uncertainty, a time of entering the unknown, and is usually characterized by chaos, stress, and anxiety. For many children, particularly those moving from another country, this stage is extremely stressful as they may not see their new home or community until they actually arrive. During this time people usually experience lower self-esteem and become more self-centered and concerned with their own needs. It is important to note that this stage does not necessarily end once we have arrived at our new destination. It only ends once we have mentally and emotionally decided to engage in the life of the new community. Some people who move actually remain in this transition stage during their entire stay in a new place as they find it difficult to take the steps to adapt.

• *Entering Stage.* The entering stage begins when we are ready to become part of life in the new place. In this stage we begin to observe new ways of doing things, take risks, and begin to reach out to others. We usually feel quite vulnerable as we learn new skills and gather new information about our new location. Emotions may fluctuate widely: We are delighted with our new life one day and feel homesick the next. It is not unusual to see some exaggerated behaviors during this stage. Children who are normally shy may become more so, and those who are outgoing may become aggressive. As we eventually adjust to life in the new place, we gain confidence and begin to feel more secure. During this stage we also go through a process of cultural adjustment. This is characterized by an initial *honeymoon period* where everything is new and exciting, followed by *culture shock* where we feel confused and disoriented in our new surroundings, and then *adjustment* where we are able to function comfortably in the new location.

• *Reinvolvement Stage.* In this last stage we finally feel settled and comfortable once again, and have a sense of place and belonging in our new community.

As you become familiar with these stages, you will be able to recognize where your students and their families are in the transition process, and you can support them accordingly. You may find that children and parents respond differently to these stages and may move through them at different rates. If you have recently moved yourself, be aware of your own responses to the transition process.

The attitudes of parents are often reflected in the attitudes of their children. It is not at all unusual for children to pick up on the stress of their parents and for them to behave differently at home than at school. Some children may have the additional burden of being responsible for interpreting the new language for their parents. Parents are often focused on the logistics of the move or on their own adjustment issues, and may overlook the emotional impact of the move on their children. Children will often share their thoughts and feelings with their teachers when they feel unable to do so with their parents. These feelings may be quite intense and should be acknowledged with empathy and understanding. As children and their families adjust to living in another culture they are likely to experience some degree of culture shock. This may be particularly difficult for some children and it is important to be aware of signs of stress. In more extreme cases these may include anxiety, irritability, aggressiveness, withdrawal, physical ailments, confusion, or depression. It may be necessary to engage the support of your principal, the school counselor, or another professional if you feel a student is experiencing extreme difficulty with transition issues.

As you explore the process of transition with your class, learn how your students have responded to the different stages. Each of us is likely to respond in our own way, and may respond differently from move to move. Children can share strategies that have worked well for them and learn from each other. Be sure to address the feelings, needs, and experiences of the children who remain behind once a friend or loved one has moved away. These children experience significant transition adjustments as well.

You may find that some children will not want to share their thoughts, feelings, and experiences for personal and/or cultural reasons. Respect this and just let them know you are there. Over time they may eventually decide to share with you or their classmates. Include a variety of opportunities for children to express their feelings about moving. Some will be more likely to share individually with a teacher, or through journals, art, music, or poetry.

CONCEPTS FEATURED IN ACTIVITIES

1. *When people move, they need to adapt to a new community and location.* There are many things to adapt to when moving to a new community. They include a new school, home, neighborhood, and possibly a new country and culture. A move to a new place requires people to adapt to new ways of doing things and new ways of being. This may include new customs,

behaviors, languages or expressions, and aspects of everyday life such as shopping, transportation, and recreation. People may also need to adapt to physical changes in their surroundings and a different climate. Let children know to expect things to be different when they move and encourage them to be open to the new experiences they encounter.

2. *Adapting to a new community is a process and involves different stages.* While it doesn't take away the stress of a move, learning about the stages of transition can ease the process for adults and children when they know what to expect. We suggest using the ADAPT model we have developed to teach your students about the process of transition and explain the stages. Talk with your students about what it means to adapt, and how people and animals adapt to their surroundings. Explain that when we move, we go through a process with different stages before we eventually adapt to our new surroundings. Teach your students about the process of transition by introducing the stages through the ADAPT model below.

ADAPT

All is well. (Involvement Stage)

Explain that in this stage we are involved in our community and feel at home where we live. We feel like we belong and "All is well."

Don't want to go, or do I? (Leaving Stage)

In this stage we first hear that we are leaving and may have many different feelings about the move. Explain that we may feel sad, angry, scared, excited, or all of these, about moving to a new place, and not be quite sure about whether or not we want to go. This stage brings many mixed emotions as we say good-bye to people and places that were important to us, and we begin to focus on the future. Our mixed feelings can be expressed as "Don't want to go, or do I?"

Anything is possible! (Transition Stage)

This stage begins when we actually leave our old home. Explain to your students that it is a time of uncertainty, and we really don't know what to expect. We may feel confused, anxious, and unsure during this time. While there are bound to be good things that happen, there will most likely be things that are unexpected too. In short, "Anything is possible!"

Perhaps this isn't so bad. (Entering Stage)

Explain to your students that once we have decided to settle in and become part of our new community, we begin to learn about life in the new place.

Things begin to look familiar, we figure out how to do things in our new school and new neighborhood, and we begin to make new friends. If we have moved to a new country, we are adjusting to new sights, smells, and foods, and are beginning to learn new customs and a new language. After awhile, as we adjust, we realize "Perhaps this isn't so bad." You can minimize the experience of culture shock that may occur in this stage by teaching your students about it. Discuss the process of cultural adaptation explaining the honeymoon, culture shock, and adaptation stages.

This is OK! (Reinvolvement Stage)

Explain that eventually we will most likely feel settled and comfortable again in the new place and will think "This is OK!"

3. *People respond differently to the experience of moving.* People respond differently to the prospect of moving for a variety of reasons. Some people are excited about an upcoming move, while others dread the thought of it, and still others have mixed feelings about moving. The differences are due to factors such as age, personality, background, expectations, adaptability, or circumstances surrounding the move such as the reasons for moving, the amount of prior notice to the move, or the destination. The number of times a person has moved also may significantly influence a person's response, and people may respond differently from move to move.

Even family members may differ in their response to moving. Some people plan to spend time with family and friends before they move, and make sure they say good-bye, while others may withdraw because it is too painful. Learning about the way we respond to new situations such as moving is part of learning more about who we are. Explain to your students that while there are many ways people respond to the experience of moving, there are things we can do to help ease the experience of moving to a new place.

4. *Cultural adaptation and culture shock are experiences of moving.* Once people arrive at a new destination, there is a process of cultural adjustment that takes place. It usually begins with a honeymoon period where everything is new and exciting as we learn about and explore our new surroundings. It is followed by the experience of culture shock. Culture shock is the disorientation we feel when cultural cues that are familiar have been taken away. Most people experience some degree of culture shock when moving to a new place, even if it is within the same country. When we are immersed in a culture where the sights, smells, sounds, foods, language, climate, and behaviors and values are all new to us, we can become quite overwhelmed. Culture shock can be minimized, however, by learning about it. Let your students know that it is normal to experience some de-

gree of culture shock when moving to a new place. While it can feel uncomfortable at first, culture shock eventually helps us to see the world in a different way. It is important to be aware of the symptoms of culture shock so you can support your students.

5. *Effective strategies for managing transition can be developed.* Moving is challenging, but there are strategies and approaches that can ease the difficulties involved in moving to a new place. Explain to your students that the process of transition can be made easier if they take the time to think about their move and plan for it. Encourage your students to learn from each other by providing opportunities for them to share their responses to moving. Explore different approaches and help your students develop their own individual strategies. Please see Appendix E, "Approaches to Transition." Examples of strategies include the following:

- Plan ahead: Find out about the place where you are moving to, know it will be different, and have realistic expectations.
- If you have questions about your move, don't be afraid to ask.
- Be patient and flexible.
- Stay focused on the present as much as possible.
- Develop rituals or traditions when you move, such as arranging your new room with your favorite things.
- Talk with your family about treasured objects you can bring with you.
- Learn to accept a degree of uncertainty, and try not to worry about the future.
- Have a sense of humor.

6. *People experience a sense of loss when they move.* It is natural to grieve when we leave people and places we love. Grieving is the healing part of loss, but it can become a problem if it is unexpressed or unresolved. It is important to allow children to grieve and discuss their sad feelings. If you are willing, model this by sharing your own experiences. Children experience simultaneous grief as they lose their home, friends, family, and special places at the same time. In some cases they also lose their pet, and this can be particularly traumatic for children. For children who move frequently, their grief may be more intense as they have had to cope with multiple moves and consequently more losses. It is important to consider whether the family as a whole has experienced a loss of social, professional, or economic status as a result of a move, and the effect that this may have on individuals within the family.

7. *People who stay behind also experience transition adjustments.* It is important to recognize that it is not just the people who move away who are affected by a move. The people who remain behind also experi-

ence significant loss when friends, family, or neighbors leave. It is important to help children realize the impact their move has on others who have been a part of their lives. It then becomes important for them to say good-bye properly and to keep in touch, for the sake of others as well as themselves.

It is also important to address the losses experienced by the children who do not move, but are constantly being left. They too need opportunities to express their feelings of sadness, loneliness, rejection, or anger and to develop strategies to cope with these feelings. Some children who stay behind become reluctant to develop new relationships, similar to the response of some of the children who frequently move. It is important to encourage them to continue to risk building new relationships. In highly transient communities such as internationals schools, help your students explore ways to develop relationships also with children who are less likely to move. This may include joining clubs or groups within the host culture.

Objectives: To provide students with the opportunity

- to learn about the different stages involved in the process of transition and the common experiences associated with them
- to explore their own responses to moving
- to learn about cultural adaptation and culture shock
- to express feelings of grief and loss
- to develop effective strategies to successfully manage transition
- to develop an awareness of the feelings of those left behind

LESSON PLAN, GRADES K–5

Alexander, Who's Not (Do you hear me? I mean it!) Going to Move by Judith Viorst

Synopsis

Alexander's dad is taking a new job, and the family has to move. While everyone else in the family, including Alexander's two older brothers, has accepted the idea of moving, Alexander has not. In fact, he maintains throughout the story that he will not move, no matter what! His parents offer suggestions to help with the transition of moving, but it isn't until the very end of the story that Alexander comes to grips with the fact that he too must move with his family to a new home.

Objectives

1. To provide students with the opportunity to gain an understanding of the process of transition and to recognize the various emotions associated with moving
2. To provide students with the opportunity to express their own feelings about a time when they had to move
3. To provide students with the opportunity to develop effective strategies to successfully manage transition
4. To provide students with the opportunity to gain an awareness of the feelings of those who stay behind

Activities Before Reading

• Before starting the story, ask if anyone ever had to move with their family to a new home, but really didn't want to go. Invite students to share their responses and memories about their own experiences.

• With the students, compile a list of emotions that people experience when they find out that they are going to move. Divide all the emotions into two separate categories, "Excited" versus "Upset." Put the list up on the board. Point out that not everyone experiences a move in the exact same way. One family member might be excited about moving, while another family member might be upset.

• Introduce the story characters by name and make up a character card for each member of Alexander's family: Mom, Dad, Nick, Anthony, and Alexander.

Activities After Reading

• After you have finished the story, hold up each character card and ask the students which category on the board it belongs in. Was the character excited or upset about moving? You might need to make a third category, "Indifferent." Once the character cards are assigned to categories, ask the students if this shows why Alexander felt so alone about not wanting to move.

• Ask if anyone can remember the three things his family offered him to help make the move easier. (He could get a dog, call his friend long distance, and sleep with his big brother the first night in the new house.) Then ask why these things would help Alexander with the move. His parents tell him some important things about leaving and moving to a new place. What do they tell him? (They tell him that he should take a last look at his special places and say good-bye to his special people, and that it might take awhile to find boys his own age and a new soccer team.) Discuss why this is important advice. Help your students think of other useful strategies to approach a move and compile an advice book for Alexander to take with him.

• Have the class compose a journal of Alexander's actual moving experience. Decide on a specific time frame, such as one week's worth of entries. Start Day 1 with "I still don't like it that we're moving!" and end the journal with "OK, so this wasn't so bad, but I am not, do you hear me, going to move again!" The entries in between can be about the physical process of packing up, driving and flying to the new location, unpacking, and so on. Talk with your students about how journals can help people validate their feelings and emotions.

• Teach your students about the process of transition through the ADAPT model described earlier in this chapter. Write the letters *A D A P T* on a chart and explain what each of the letters and stages in the ADAPT model mean. Ask your students where they think Alexander is in the transition process and how he is responding to it. He is in the "Don't want to go, or do I?" stage (Leaving Stage). The entire book takes place in this stage, since Alexander clearly does not want to move although he eventually comes to accept the inevitable. Compare his reaction to this stage to that of his brothers and parents.

• Alexander experiences several different feelings which can be can be seen in his face. Go back through the book on a "picture walk" and ask your class to raise their hands whenever Alexander's facial expressions change. Ask them to identify the feelings.

• Alexander's classmates and teacher gave him "moving gifts" to show that they would miss him. Brainstorm what kind of items your students could put into a backpack that would be an appropriate moving gift for someone who has to move away from your school. Now brainstorm a different type of gift, a "welcome gift." What type of items could you put together that would welcome a new student to your class and help ease the transition of moving into a new school?

Suggested Follow-up Activities

• Have your students interview their family members about their reactions to a recent move or their feelings about the experience of moving in general. Provide an opportunity to share the interviews with the class. Help the children see that members of their own family may respond differently to moving, just as in Alexander's family.

• For highly mobile children, discuss whether it gets easier or harder with each move. Why?

• It's important for students to understand that the friends they leave behind also have an adjustment to the moving experience. Have students extend the ending of Alexander's story and write a few more pages told from his best friend's point of view on how he feels about Alexander's moving away.

• Many of your students may have experienced both leaving and being left behind. Provide an opportunity for them to share their feelings about both experiences. Teach your students how to compose a "Double entry diary." Take a sheet of paper and divide it in half vertically. In the left-side column students are to write about what it is like when they move away. Then on the right side of the page ask them to write about their own reaction when they are left behind when a friend moves away. Children who have not moved can write about what it would be like for them in both situations, or the benefits and challenges of staying versus leaving. Comment on the diary entries your students have completed to validate their feelings.

Transition Education Links

This story has links with objectives in Chapter 2, "The Common Experience of Mobility." Alexander is worried that he will never again have a best friend like Paul, or a great sitter like Rachel, or his soccer team or car pool, or kids who know him. Provide an opportunity for your students to express the worries and concerns they had when they moved to the place they are now living.

This story also links with objectives in Chapter 5, "Friendships and Relationships." Ask students to think of ways that Alexander might try to find a new friend in the school he will attend. Since Alexander is a soccer player perhaps he can find someone in his new class who also plays soccer. Ask your students to share ways they make new friends or could make new friends.

This story has links with objectives in Chapter 6, "Problem-Solving Skills." Ask students to make a list of all the special places Alexander went to, to say good-bye. Ask students to make their own good-bye list of who or what they would want to visit one last time before moving. Have students share their lists with each other and discuss why they picked the people or places they did. This provides students with the opportunity to share ideas of how to say good-bye to their old home, school, and community. For immigrant and refugee children and other children who might not have had the opportunity to say good-bye, discuss how they might say good-bye in their mind's eye.

LESSON PLAN, GRADES 3–5

Dandelions
by Eve Bunting

Synopsis

This is the story of the westward movement and a family who leaves their home in Illinois to stake a claim out on the Nebraska prairie. While Papa is very excited about the move, his wife is already missing their familiar home back in Illinois, and his two daughters are anxious about what life on the prairie will be like. At the end of the story, the older daughter, Zoe, discovers some dandelions growing at the edge of town and takes them back to their house on the prairie. The transplanted dandelions become a metaphor for the transplanted family, and it isn't until then that both Mama and the girls realize that it will take time for all of them to adjust to this new life.

Objectives

1. To provide students with the opportunity to understand that adapting to a new home is a process and takes time
2. To provide students with the opportunity to understand that people, even within the same family, respond differently to moving to a new home
3. To provide students with the opportunity to learn more about cultural adaptation and culture shock
4. To provide students with the opportunity to become aware of the feelings of those left behind

Activities Before Reading

• Write the word *transplanted* on the board, and ask your students to define it. Then ask for examples of sentences that use the word in context to explain its meaning. Using the analogy of gardening, brainstorm with the class which plants are the easiest to transplant and why. Usually plants that are hardy and are transplanted to an environment conducive to growth are the ones that survive. It is also easier to transplant plants that do not have strong roots. Then talk about plants that are difficult to transplant. These would be the fragile variety, or ones that need special growing conditions in order to survive. Plants that are root bound are also difficult to transplant.

Ask your students in what ways people who move to a new location are like plants. They too can be transplanted out of their familiar surroundings and into a new environment. The roots they have in a particular place also affect the impact of a move. Ask your students what qualities help plants survive in a new place (strength, flexibility, and adaptability). Are these the same qualities that could apply to people as well?

Activities After Reading

• Discuss the idea of the characters in this story being transplanted. Which characters were adapting to being transplanted and which character was having the most difficult time with the move? Why do they suppose it was easier for Papa and the girls to begin adjusting to their new life, and harder for Mama? (Papa was delighted that they could at last own their own land and the young daughters had not yet developed strong roots to their Illinois home. Mama, on the other hand, was leaving her parents and all she knew behind.) Discuss why it may be harder for the parents in immigrant and refugee families to adjust than the children.

• Explain that the family, particularly the mother, was probably experiencing some degree of culture shock when they moved to Nebraska. Explain that culture shock is a sense of disorientation that people experience when the sights, smells, sounds, and way of life is very different from what they were used to or have experienced before. Help your students identify some of the factors that would contribute to this in the story. (There were not many trees; the open prairie was empty; everything looked the same; the town and the neighbors were far away; they were used to a house with wallpaper and china plates; and there weren't all the different flowers they were used to seeing.) Ask your students in what ways they may have experienced culture shock in moving to the place they live now. Point out that culture shock can occur even if you are moving within the same country or visiting another culture vastly different than your own. Nonmobile children can relate culture shock to places they may have visited.

Because all human emotions are a result of cause and effect stimuli, put a "Cause and Effect" chart up on the board and as a class fill in the appropriate answers. Start with listing a "cause event" and have the students give the resulting "effect." See how many events in the story caused a character to feel a particular emotion about moving. A sample chart is given in Figure 3.1.

• Even though Mama is sad at having to leave her family behind, the family is embarking on an exciting move, to a brand-new life. Imagine how Mama's parents felt at seeing their daughter, son-in-law, and grandchildren moving so far away and to a place that was unknown to them. Have your

FIGURE 3.1. Cause and Effect

Cause	Effect
Father wanted to own land	The family moved to Nebraska
They do not have close neighbors	Mama is lonely
There are a few trees on the prairie	They build a sod house to live in
Zoe plants dandelions on the roof	Mama realizes adjusting takes time

students write a letter to Mama from her parents, so that she gets some familiar news from home and knows that they miss her too. Acknowledge that for immigrant or refugee children, their families may have had a strong response to their leaving, especially if they left suddenly. Immigrant and refugee children can write their own letters to family telling them about life in the new place. Help your students recognize that the people who stay behind also have to adjust to the move.

Suggested Follow-up Activities

• Review the concept of a time line. Together with your students first create a time line of significant events in a typical school day. This would include getting up, getting dressed, eating breakfast, catching the school bus, going to school, doing homework, playing with a friend, eating dinner, reading, and going to sleep. Have your students then work with a partner to create a time line for the family in this story, identifying the significant events in their move to Nebraska. These could include traveling in the wagon, crossing the rivers, arriving at their plot of land, meeting the Svensons, digging the well, building their house, going in to town the first time, and, of course, planting the dandelions! You can use this opportunity to teach your students about the process of transition and relate these events to the stages in the ADAPT model. Most of these events take place in the "Anything is possible!" stage (Transition Stage), and once the house is built and the dandelions are planted, the family is beginning to move into the "Perhaps this isn't so bad" stage (Entering Stage).

Students can then create a time line noting the significant events in their move to the place they are living now. These events might include moving to their house, the first day at their new school, making a new friend, finding their way around town, and so on. Help them see that all of these events are a part of the process of settling in to a new place and represent their unique experience doing so.

Transition Education Links

This story has links with objectives in Chapter 2, "The Common Experience of Mobility." The mother feels a sense of loss from leaving her well-loved home in Illinois. Provide an opportunity for your students to empathize with her and share their feelings about moving from a place that was special in their lives.

Color is an important theme in this story because the prairie seemed to be one endless stretch of green, and Mama missed the colors of the flowers from her previous home. Tell your students that you want them to think of one important color from their home vicinity, where they live now, or a place they have lived before. Then using a large wall-size piece of bulletin board paper construct a "color memory mural" for your room. Divide the mural into enough sections so that each student, and you, will have a space to both paint and write. Ask the students to paint any color in their space that evokes a memory of their home. Underneath the paint ask them to write what the color represents and their name. No pictures are to be painted, just large swatches of colors. For example, a student may paint a vibrant swatch of yellow and write, "This is the color of the sunflowers in Arles, France, where I was born." Remind students of the last page in the story and how the yellow of the dandelions was the prominent color to help Mama remember her other home. When you are finished, this Color Memory Mural will be an artistic rendition of the colors of various places in the world where all of you have lived and represent those special memories.

Identify the new skills the family learned as a result of their move to Nebraska. These include planting crops, building a sod house, digging a well, and figuring out direction without man-made landmarks. Help your students identify the new skills they have learned as a result of a move they have made.

This story also links to Chapter 5, "Friendships and Relationships." Friendships are an important part of moving and when Mama meets Mrs. Svenson for the first time the girls are surprised at how quickly the two women become friends. Why was this friendship so important to the two women? (Because there were so few women on the prairie.) What had the two women left behind that made them feel like they had lost a part of their lives? (They had left behind an extended family of grandparents, cousins, and others that they might never see again.) How did the Svensons become more than just neighbors? (They helped Papa by lending him tools and promising to help him build his own house.)

Ask your students to suggest ways in which Zoe and her sister might become stronger friends with the Svenson boys. Ask your students to share effective ways they make new friends and the qualities they look for in a friend.

The story links with Chapter 6, "Problem-Solving Skills" as it provides an opportunity to discuss ways the family could approach change and ease their transition. These could include enjoying what there is on the prairie such as the beautiful sunsets, looking for wildflowers to create a garden, visiting the Svensons more often or inviting them to visit, and reminiscing about their old home as well. Have your students explore the ways they approached their move to the place they are living now.

Zoe is already being resourceful with her idea of the dandelions as a solution to Mama's missing her flower garden from home, and Papa is thinking ahead about getting Mama a real window so the sod house will seem more comfortable. What other ideas can your students problem-solve that would make the sod house more inviting? Remember there is no electricity and the girls have limited resources, but what could be done?

LESSON PLAN, GRADES K–5

Scrumpy
by Elizabeth Dale

Synopsis

Ben's dog, Scrumpy, is a very special friend. They go everywhere together. One day Scrumpy gets sick and soon dies. This story sensitively describes Ben's feelings of grief and loss. There will never be another Scrumpy! As time passes, Ben is able to remember Scrumpy fondly and is eventually ready to get another dog. Even though Honey is special too, she will never take Scrumpy's place. This touching story comprehensively addresses grief and loss issues with children and is an excellent springboard to discuss many issues related to moving.

Objectives

1. To provide students with the opportunity to recognize that people respond differently to the experience of moving and to explore their own responses
2. To provide students with the opportunity to express and explore feelings of grief and loss associated with moving

Activities Before Reading

• Share your own background with your students. Ask them to share the place where they were born and how long they lived there, and any other countries or places they have lived. Some of your students may have moved to another house, yet have stayed in the same city or town, while others may never have moved at all. Affirm each child's unique experience.

• Acknowledge the mobility and international makeup in your class. Let the children know that one thing some of them have in common is that they have moved at least once and are living in a place or country different from the one where they were born. Ask your students to think about their last move to the place they live now or a previous move. Ask, "What was it like for you first hearing the news, then preparing to leave, and actually moving?" Your students will likely be eager to share their experiences.

• Discuss and chart the benefits and challenges they see in moving to and living in another place or country. This will also prove useful for other activities at another time. If you have students in your class who have not moved, include their experience and find ways they can contribute as well. Perhaps they can share what it is like to constantly be the one who stays behind when others leave, or they can discuss the benefits and challenges of having mobile classmates.

It is important to be aware that these discussions may evoke strong feelings and may be the first time your students have had an opportunity to share them. Simply allow your students to express their feelings, and let them know you understand how they feel. Explain that it is natural to feel sad about leaving people and places you love or having others leave you, and tears are a normal response as well as a healing one. If children left their home under extreme circumstances, their memories may be particularly painful to recall.

Activities After Reading

• Encourage the children's personal responses to the story. They will probably share stories of pets, family members, or friends who have died. Acknowledge their feelings. Ask them, "What is the author telling us about losing something we love?" Discuss their responses.

• The feelings Ben experiences are similar to those in the transition process associated with moving. Ask your students to think about how the story about Scrumpy relates to moving. Discuss this and pose questions if necessary to establish the similarities. They include the following:

• Ben's feelings of sadness and anger in losing Scrumpy are some of the same feelings we may have when we leave a place we love.
• It took time for Ben to feel better and often takes time to settle into a new place.

- Although Honey did not take Scrumpy's place, and the new country or location does not take the place of our old home or the last one we left, we can appreciate more than one place as there are special things about each of them.
- Ben's memories were painful at first and then became happier, which may happen when we move from one place to another.

Chart the children's responses.

    • Discuss the following with your students: "We have been talking about moving. Why do you think it is an important topic to discuss?" (Moving involves many big changes in our lives, and it is important to understand the ways they may affect us.) Acknowledge their responses.

    • Introduce the idea of sharing our experiences of moving in a class book. The possibilities are endless! One suggestion is to have each child contribute a page with the following pattern:

    Before I moved I . . .
    Now that I have moved I . . .
    Next time I move . . .

Have the students develop one response for each sentence that is most meaningful for them and illustrate the final page. Students can write a paragraph for each sentence starter or simply complete the sentence depending on their age and English proficiency. This activity works well with children who are learning English as another language. It can also be modified for children who have not moved. They can complete a page as follows:

    When friends move I . . .
    When new students arrive I . . .
    If I move I . . .

Don't forget to include your own page! Share the finished book.

Suggested Follow-up Activities

    • Have students design a feelings questionnaire and survey faculty and students in your school to find out about the different ways people have responded to moving in your school community.

    • Ben had a good cry and for a long while all he could think about was Scrumpy. While it is natural to feel sad for awhile, Ben did different things to take his mind off missing Scrumpy. Have your students explore effective ways to manage their feelings of sadness and loneliness and find ways that work for them. These may include talking to a parent, brother, or sister; keeping a journal; cuddling a favorite stuffed animal; reading a good book; or drawing a picture.

Transition Education Links

This story has links with Chapter 2, "The Common Experience of Mobility." Ben is eventually reminded of the joyful times he and Scrumpy had, and for the first time he is glad for all they had shared together. Ask your students to consider the good times they had in other places they have lived. Have them construct a memory mobile with pictures or photographs of the special people and places that are part of their past. They might choose to include current photographs or pictures as well to show the memories they are making where they live now.

LESSON PLAN, GRADES K–3

We Are Best Friends
by Aliki

Synopsis

Robert and Peter are best friends; and when Peter moves away, Robert is sad and lonely. Both boys eventually make a new friend, but they don't forget each other and keep in touch through letters. This story addresses the feelings of those who are left behind, and also shows us that friendships can continue after a friend has moved away.

Objectives

1. To provide students with the opportunity to develop an awareness of the feelings of those left behind
2. To provide students with the opportunity to develop effective strategies to manage transition
3. To provide students with the opportunity to express feelings of grief and loss

Activities Before Reading

• Discuss the qualities of true friendship. Are these qualities that can keep a friendship alive even if one of the friends moves away? What makes a person a best friend?
• Ask the students if they have ever had a friend who has moved away. Invite them to share how they felt about it and what they did, if

anything, to feel better. Are they still in touch with those friends? Explain that this story has some important messages about making a friend, keeping a friend, and being a friend.

Activities After Reading

• How did Robert feel when Peter left? Relate this to the children's experiences they shared earlier. Robert is so sad and angry that at first he ignores Will, who is new in his class, and he doesn't play with the other children. Ask the children why they think he acts this way. Point out that this is a response to grief and loss. After he gets Peter's letter he realizes that Will is new, just like Peter, and that he is probably also feeling lonely. Robert is feeling lonely too! Encourage your students to share their feelings when they or a friend moved away, and acknowledge their sense of loss.

• When Peter wrote to Robert, he told him that he liked his new house and new school now, although at first he didn't like anything. Now he also has a friend named Alex. Explain to your students that it takes time to settle into a new place and that, like Peter, at first they may not like anything either. Making a new friend usually changes things for us just as meeting Alex was the turning point for Peter, and now he wasn't so lonely. Remind your students that whether they are moving or staying behind, they can reach out and make new friends to help them feel less lonely. Acknowledge that this takes courage and involves taking a risk. Explain that sometimes children who move may not want to reach out again, as it is painful to make friends and then lose them. Help your students to see the value of forming friendships no matter how long they last.

• In the story Robert worries that Peter doesn't even remember him. Peter worries about the same thing. Explain that this is a common worry that people have when they move away or a friend moves. Encourage your students to take the initiative to keep old friendships alive.

• Robert sees Will when he is out riding his bike and starts a conversation with him. Discuss ways to start a conversation with someone you don't know. How can you find out if you have common interests? What are some things you could teach or share with another child? Have your students learn more about their own interests. Ask them to complete a list of "Twenty Things I Like to Do." Then have them work with a partner to role-play initiating a conversation and an activity with a new person in their class or neighborhood.

Suggested Follow-up Activities

• Even though Robert became friends with Will, and Peter became friends with Alex, they still wrote to each other. Their letters were personal and let the other person know that even though he had made a new friend, his old friend still had a special place in his life. Discuss the qualities of a good letter. Institute a yearlong letter writing project with your class. Have students choose a friend or relative from their home country or one of the places they have lived to correspond with. Have students write to this person explaining that their class will be writing to their special friends once a month. Students can design their own stationery and include drawings, photographs or poems with their letters. Some of your students may wish to write to a friend in another language. Invite them to share the letters they receive and designate a bulletin board to celebrate their friends around the world. Nonmobile children can write to a friend or relative who lives elsewhere. Also participate in this project yourself. This provides children with the experience of keeping in touch with others after they have moved.

• What could the other children in the class have done to help make Robert feel better? Ask, "Have you ever reached out to a new child in your class or neighborhood? What have you done or could you do to make the person feel less lonely?" Have your students compile their ideas and create a manual on "How to Reach Out to Others."

Transition Education Links

This story has links with objectives in Chapter 5, "Friendships and Relationships." It provides an opportunity for children to further explore ways to choose and make new friends. Robert and Peter keep in touch through writing letters and plan to visit each other during the summer. Explore other ways that friendships can continue after someone moves away.

For children who have moved frequently, discuss ways they can keep in touch with friends from several different places. Discuss how they decide which friends to keep in touch with and which friendships to let go.

It also can be used to help children develop empathy for those who are staying behind and those who are arriving in a new community. The other children must have been aware that Robert was sad and missing Peter. Discuss ways they could have reached out to him and helped him to feel better such as talking to him and including him in their games. Have your students role-play a conversation with Robert letting him know that they know how he feels. Ask your students to share ways they can and do reach out to others, or times others have reached out to them.

LESSON PLAN, GRADES 4–5

In the Year of the Boar and Jackie Robinson
by Bette Bao Lord

Synopsis

　　This is the story of a young girl who leaves her native China to come and live in Brooklyn, New York, in 1947. At first her story is similar to many immigrant children: She has difficulty making new friends, learning a new language, and adjusting to a new life in a new country that is so different from the life she led before. But then a uniquely American experience—baseball—changes forever her feelings of being a foreigner in a foreign land.

Objectives

1. To provide students with the opportunity to learn about the different stages involved in moving and the common experiences associated with them
2. To provide students with the opportunity to learn about cultural adaptation and culture shock
3. To provide students with the opportunity to express feelings of grief and loss for the home and life they left behind
4. To provide students with the opportunity to develop effective strategies to successfully manage transition

Activities Before Reading

　　• Ask how many students in your classroom have had to move from one country to another. Then ask how many students have had to learn a new language because of a move to another country. Count the number of hands each time and tabulate the number of students in your class who have had this experience. Then ask those students to share what they felt was the most difficult part of learning to live in an entirely new country or having to learn a new language. As students share their responses, post their experiences on the board.
　　• Then write the word *ambassador* on the board and explain that an ambassador is a representative from one country who goes to live and work in another country. Ambassadors represent the people of their home country. Give each student a large index card and have him or her fold it in half so it sits on each student's desk as a nameplate. Next have them write the name of their home country on the card. On the back of the card have them

write the following three things: a favorite food from their country, a favorite game that students in their country play, and the authentic spelling
of their birth name. Give each student an opportunity to reintroduce him
or herself as an ambassador from his or her home country, sharing the information on the back of the nameplate. Students who have never moved
should make nameplates as well. Explain that in this story the main character feels like an ambassador from her country.

Activities After Reading

- Teach your students about the process of transition by presenting
the ADAPT model. Put the letters *A D A P T* on the board and explain what
each letter and stage represents. Then initiate a class discussion about the
different stages and see if the students can identify when in the story Shirley
Temple Wong experienced them. Each chapter represents another month
in the year of her move, so you can create a time line with your class of
when the stages in the ADAPT model occurred during the year.

- *All is well.* This stage starts in January when Shirley is still living in China
  with her large extended family. Ask the students for examples of the
  things that made her happy in her home and life there.
- *Don't want to go, or do I?* This stage also happens in January when Shirley
  at first does not want to move to America, but then begins to get excited
  about the prospect of moving. Choosing her American name is the definitive event of this chapter.
- *Anything is possible!* This stage begins in February as Shirley's family
  moves to New York City. Ask the students to recall the actual trip to
  America. Did it meet Shirley's expectations? How did Shirley react once
  she and her family got to their new apartment? Have the students explain Shirley's initial reactions of disappointment.
- *Perhaps this isn't so bad.* It usually takes a while to enter this stage, and
  for Shirley it doesn't happen until she discovers baseball and the other
  children begin to accept her into their peer group. This begins in May
  and continues until September when Shirley is fearful of school starting again and that her friends from last year may have changed.
- *This is OK!* This stage occurs from October on, when Shirley realizes that
  America is truly home now, and it isn't bad at all. A shared love of baseball is what helps her to make new friends and adjust to her new life in
  America. However, it isn't until the end of the story when Shirley starts
  to plan all the wonderful things she is going to teach her future baby
  brother, who will be born an American, that she realizes how happy she
  is in her new country.

Have your students work in pairs and assign one month from the story to each group. Ask them to identify the most memorable event of that month, and then have the whole class see how that event relates to the ADAPT model.

• Remind your students of the concept of ambassadorship. In what ways was it a burden for Shirley Temple Wong to feel that she was an ambassador for her country? (She was always afraid that she was making a mistake and did not want to appear foolish.) How did those feelings add to her stress of making the transition to a new life in America? (Life in Brooklyn was already confusing because it was so different from her life in China.)

• When Shirley first arrived in New York she began to experience culture shock because it was so different from Chungking. Reread pages 27 and 28 to your students and ask them to recall Shirley's first impressions. (It was Sunday so the streets were empty, the buildings were so tall she couldn't see the roofs, there were no bicycles, rickshaws, mules, or carts, no peddlers or farmers' stalls, and all the buildings looked alike.) Ask the students to share their first impressions of the new community in which they now live.

• Continue with a discussion of culture shock. This was the first time Shirley and her mother had seen an icebox or a washing machine. There were no hills or gardens, and everyone looked different to Shirley. Provide an opportunity for your students to share their experiences of culture shock.

• Sometimes when a family moves to another country, their lifestyle changes dramatically. For instance, a father might have been a professional in his home country, but finds he cannot get the same kind of work in the new country. Or a mother may have had domestic help in her home country, but now must do all the housework herself. How would these two scenarios make the adjustment even more difficult for a family, particularly an immigrant or refugee family?

• Both Shirley and her mother demonstrated a positive approach to the transition to the new culture. When Mrs. Wong realized there were no servants, she said, "Well then, I shall learn to cook and shop." Shirley was curious about her new neighborhood and the new culture. She took risks like going to the store for her father and trying out some of the new behaviors she observed and language she heard. Discuss other positive strategies to approach the transition to life in a new country and encourage your students to share those they have found effective.

• Part of learning to adapt to life in a new country is learning the social skills that help you to be accepted by your peers. Ask your students if they have ever heard the phrase "Sticks and stones can break my bones, but names can never hurt me." Ask them if they believe that to be true, that names can never hurt. Pose this question, "Why do you think children sometimes call each other hurtful names?" "Why are newcomers sometimes singled out?" Ask if anyone in the class has ever experienced this, and ask them to share how they felt. Then ask them their opinions about how Shirley handled the situation when other children made fun of her at the stickball game. Could Shirley have tried different tactics?

> • Ask your students to think back to the part where Shirley winks at everyone on her first day of school because the principal had winked at her. She was observing a new behavior and trying to adopt it herself. Ask the students to brainstorm ways in which Shirley, or any new student, could go about acclimating themselves to a new culture. What would be some positive strategies for a person to use in order to make new friends? It might be helpful to list the strategies that Shirley tried, then have your students comment on the often funny results that she first encountered, as follows:

- Learn the new language as quickly as possible. (At first it sounded like gurgling water.)
- Try the new food that you see everyone else eating. (She wasn't used to the sandwiches other students ate.)
- Try to learn the sports or activities that are popular in the new country. (She became a baseball fan.)

Ask your highly mobile students who have had to make new friends often if there are any strategies they have found particularly useful.

> • Baseball became the shared interest that helped Shirley make friends with the other children in her class. Ask your students to list their favorite pastimes, and then lead a discussion about how they could make friends with someone who enjoys the same pastime they do.

Suggested Follow-up Activities

> • When there were times in the story when Shirley felt sad or lonely or even angry, she often wrote letters back to her cousins in China. Encourage your students to start a "Feelings" page in their journals and to write in them any time they experience strong feelings because of their move or a friend's move. Start them off with a sample from the book. Shirley felt sad when she realized that they had forgotten to celebrate the traditions of the Mid-Autumn Festival. "How could they have let the eve of Mid-Autumn Festival slip by without realizing it? Americans did not commemorate the fullest moon of the year, but the Wongs had done so for centuries."

(p. 150). Periodically respond to their journal entries and plan times when students can share their responses out loud with their classmates.

Transition Education Links

This story has transition links to Chapter 4, "Personal and Cultural Identity." Have your students take a look at which Chinese traditions the Wongs continued to observe once they started their new life in America. Ask your students to share which customs your students and their families share from their passport countries. Ask if anyone's family has a special tradition that follows them from place to place, like arranging family mementos in a certain area of each new home. Ask your highly mobile students if there are traditions from several different countries that have become part of their lives.

Even though Shirley adapted to life in America, she realized she must never forget China or lose her Chinese. Encourage your students to share the ways they stay connected to their culture. It may be through keeping in touch with friends and family back home, reading books and newspapers in their native language, continuing lessons in their mother tongue, or displaying photographs of their home country in their rooms.

This story also has links with Chapter 5, "Friendships and Relationships." Shirley knows what it is like to be new. Discuss the ways she reached out to the new student, Emily, and developed a friendship with her. Ask your students to suggest ways they can reach out to others who are new to the community and discuss effective skills for making new friends.

IDEAS FOR CROSS-CURRICULAR CONNECTIONS

Creative and Performing Arts

Encourage students to write poems expressing their feelings about the transitions involved in moving to a new home. Then host an "open mike" where students can voluntarily read their poetry aloud to their peers. These poems can then be displayed in two unique ways. First, you can draw the outline of a large tree on mural paper. Cut it out and attach it to your wall. Then have students attach their poems all over the tree, which then becomes a "poet-tree." Another way is to stretch a length of clothesline across the classroom and have the students "hang out" their poems by attaching them with clothes pins.

In the story *In the Year of the Boar and Jackie Robinson*, Shirley blinks in response to the wink the principal gives her when she arrives. She continues to blink at others as a sign of friendship, and eventually her teacher suggests she should have her eyes checked. Most of us make embarrassing mistakes as part of adapting to a new culture. Have your students work in small groups to write and perform short skits that illustrate the humorous side to culture learning that people might experience when they arrive in a new place. For example, they may order something in a restaurant only to find it has no resemblance to what they thought it would be. Or they may misunderstand gestures or confuse greetings, such as moving to kiss someone on the cheek as the person reaches out to shake hands. Encourage your students to draw on any personal experiences with culture shock as they develop their scene.

Social Studies

Moving almost always involves learning to find your way around in a new area. Help your students learn how to read a map. Show them where to locate the legend, the scale, and the compass rose. Then teach them how to use those tools. It is useful for students to be familiar with where the continents and oceans are located on a world map, as well as the countries they have lived in. Give each child a local map of the community and help them to locate reference points like a library, hospital, school, and so on. Include a search for monuments, museums, and other points of interest as well.

Science

One of the main experiences in moving to a new area is trying new types of food that are popular in the new community. Add to your students' knowledge of healthy habits by doing a take-off on the traditional food pyramid and identify popular local foods in terms of the food groups in which they belong. Is an item mostly a grain, a vegetable or fruit, a meat, or a sweet? Or does it fall into several categories? Have your students plan a healthy menu for a day including local produce and specialities. Help them see that by eating many different types of foods, they can make healthy choices when eating foods in any culture.

Math

Money can be a perplexing problem, especially when students move to different countries and must switch currency as well. Although the new

Euro makes this problem easier in parts of Europe, there are still many areas of the world where money must be exchanged and an entire new language learned for its value. Make up some paper money from different countries and help your students learn the names for the different currencies as well as their values. You can get this current information easily from the Internet. If possible, have children bring in different currencies from places they have lived. Your students can compare the attributes of the different bills and coins.

Chapter 4

Personal and Cultural Identity

Each one of us is unique. Our identity, or sense of self, is formed by our own individual combination of personal characteristics and life experiences. Our personal identity and cultural identity are inextricably linked. While we all have individual personality traits and temperaments, the cultures we grow up in significantly influence our identity.

Children first learn about culture from their families and the communities in which they live. Culture is a shared way of life that includes values, beliefs, attitudes, behaviors, and customs, and is passed on from one generation to the next. Culture is expressed in the food we eat, the clothes we wear, the ways we behave, the traditions we follow, our religious practices, and the festivals we celebrate. All of these aspects of culture reflect our underlying values and what is important to us. It is through our culture that we develop our perception of what is right or wrong, good or bad, beautiful or ugly.

L. Robert Kohls (1996) developed a model of a "cultural iceberg" that is helpful in understanding the dimensions of culture (see Figure 4.1). The aspects of culture that are most readily apparent, such as words, behavior, customs, and traditions, appear above the water. Below the water lie the deeper aspects of culture that one learns by careful observation and understanding. These include beliefs, values, assumptions, and thought processes.

It is important to help children learn to take pride in their cultural heritage and see the value and richness in the cultures of others as well.

Explore the differences that exist in gestures, such as greeting someone. Do you kiss, bow, or shake hands? In some cultures people kiss once on the cheek, yet in others it may be two or even three times. Others may hug or pat each other on the shoulder. Use of eye contact may also differ from culture to culture. In many cultures it is respectful to use direct eye contact when speaking to someone, while in others it is considered polite to avert one's eyes. There are many different ways of eating as well. Some people use a fork and knife, while others may use chopsticks or eat with their hands.

FIGURE 4.1. Cultural Iceberg (L. Robert Kohls)

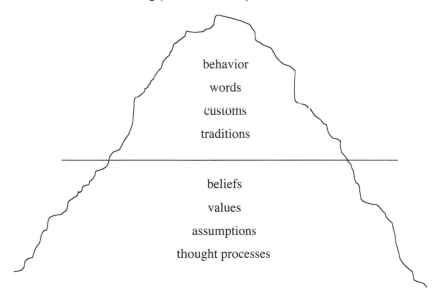

The important thing is to teach children to observe difference and foster an openness about learning how and why people do what they do. Cultural differences are often regarded as threatening, but with openness and understanding they can be enriching.

There are many cultural influences on the lives of all children. Children may be influenced by the cultures of baby-sitters, teachers, friends, neighbors, and other people who are or have been significant in their lives. Children from bicultural families are often raised with the traditions and beliefs of more than one culture. For example, children with an Indian mother and a Dutch father may see himself or herself as both Indian and Dutch to varying degrees. If the parents are bicultural themselves, there may be additional cultural influences.

Children who move are influenced by the cultures of the places they live or even visit. Experiencing life in another place gives them an understanding of another way people live. Their cultural identity may or may not coincide with their national identity if they have grown up outside of their home country. For example, an American child living in Japan may identify more strongly with the Japanese culture than the American one. Even when that child moves away from Japan, he or she may always identify with some aspects of the Japanese culture.

Some children who move internationally may identify with their passport country, the country or countries where their parents were born, or a particular country or countries where they have lived and feel a strong connection. Or they may see themselves as having a sense of belonging to the many countries and cultures they have lived in.

Children who have lived in different countries may see themselves as multicultural if they have internalized the practices and values of two or more cultures. A French child growing up in Israel and Kenya may identify with all three cultures. Some children may have a different cultural identity than their parents, and some of the students you teach may have a different cultural identity than you have, even though you share the same nationality. Demonstrate an interest in learning about your students' unique backgrounds and learn how they view themselves. Are they Japanese? Austrian? Brazilian? Maori? Kurdish? Jewish? Moslem? Or are they a combination of cultures? It is important for you to learn how your students identify themselves so you will understand the cultural differences that arise in the classroom.

You may find that some children switch from one language and culture at school to another at home. Other children are so eager to fit in with their peers that they reject their own culture and want to assimilate into the new one. You can play a positive role in helping your students take pride in their own cultural backgrounds and see the value of sharing their heritage while supporting their desire to adapt to the new culture of the country in which they are living. It is important to note that it is sometimes the parents who encourage their children to assimilate and deny their own culture.

It is important to provide opportunities for all children to explore who they are and help them come to know themselves and their classmates. Help children learn to take pride in their cultural heritage and to see the value and richness in the cultures of others as well. Find ways to celebrate their unique backgrounds in all aspects of the curriculum. Provide opportunities in your classroom for creating self-awareness, so children can begin to experience and develop their own identity. Provide opportunities for them to learn more about their strengths and weaknesses, learning styles, interests, passions, what they are curious about, and what is important to them. Help your students become more aware of their feelings and values, and validate who they are as individuals. This will help them develop inner confidence and positive self-esteem, and will enable them to fully develop their potential and lead meaningful lives.

Integrate opportunities to learn about different cultures throughout the curriculum. Make sure your classroom reflects the diversity of your students *and* our world. Include books, magazines, newspapers, artifacts, toys, games, and art from many cultures, and incorporate learning activities where students can learn about and share in each other's cultures and languages in authentic ways. Consider ways to include your students' parents as resources for culture learning in the classroom.

Children learn important values in the school environment, and it is therefore important for their teachers to exemplify a genuine respect and appreciation for all cultures.

CONCEPTS FEATURED IN ACTIVITIES

1. *Culture is at the core of our being.* Culture is learned from our very first interactions with our world and is an important part of who we are. Culture influences the way we think, the way we behave, the way we speak, and the way we live our lives. As children explore their own cultural practices, they learn more about themselves and can begin to understand the cultural practices of others.

2. *We bring our knowledge and understanding of other places we have lived with us wherever we go.* The cultures of the places we live in have an impact on our lives. Children who move develop an understanding of different ways of thinking and being, and different ways of doing things. They acquire knowledge of different cultures, and all of this broadens their understanding of the world and helps them learn to appreciate the unique cultural identities of others.

3. *The experiences we have had are part of who we are.* All of our life experiences help shape our identity and help define how we see ourselves and how we interact with our world. Children who move and experience cultural differences often develop new interests and adopt certain practices into their lifestyle. For example, a child living in England may develop a love of playing cricket, or a child living in Japan may remove his or her shoes before entering the house. Educators can help children see how these experiences help them know more about the world and enrich their lives.

4. *Our cultural identity frames our personal identity and helps shape our thinking and perception of the world around us.* The values we are taught during childhood directly affect the beliefs we hold and the way we see the world. While we all have individual personalities and characteristics, culture is at the very core of our being.

5. *There is great value in learning about other people's cultures.* We live in a world that is wonderfully diverse. Each culture has something special to offer and adds richness and depth to our experience of the world. By demonstrating your own curiosity about other cultures, you can foster a desire in your students to learn about them as well.

6. *Understanding and accepting cultural differences is an important life skill.* Understanding cultural differences fosters cross-cultural communication as children learn that we can express ourselves in different ways and look at situations from many perspectives. Cultural understanding promotes harmony and cooperation between people and communities, which is essential to a peaceful world. You can begin to develop important cross-cultural skills with your students by fostering an understanding of the cultural differences that exist in your classroom.

7. *When we experience other cultures, we come to understand our own culture more deeply.* Most of our culture learning is unconscious. We are often unaware of elements of our own culture until we are faced with different ways of doing things. It is through learning about another culture that we become more aware of cultural differences and begin to understand them. Life in the classroom provides many rich opportunities for children to learn about each other's cultures and consequently their own.

Objectives: To provide students with the opportunity

- to understand what culture is and how it is learned
- to explore the cultural influences in their lives
- to gain a greater sense of self-awareness and understanding of their own cultural identity
- to gain an appreciation of their cultural or multicultural selves
- to share their cultural backgrounds and knowledge of other cultures they have experienced
- to develop cross-cultural awareness and sensitivity
- to develop an appreciation and respect for cultural diversity

LESSON PLAN, GRADES K–5

Stellaluna
by Janell Cannon

Synopsis

Stellaluna is a fruit bat who becomes separated from her mother one night and falls into a bird nest. Left to live with the birds, she adapts to their way of life, and learns to fly by day and eat bugs. Although she learns how to adapt, she never loses her bat ways completely. She is eventually reunited with her mother and rediscovers her unique "batness." Stellaluna returns to visit the bird friends she has made, and they all discover that although they are different, they are friends!

Objectives

1. To provide students with the opportunity to gain a greater sense of self-awareness and understanding of their cultural identity
2. To provide students with the opportunity to gain an understanding of culture and how it is learned
3. To provide students with the opportunity to explore the cultural influences in their lives
4. To provide students with the opportunity to learn about the cultures of their classmates and develop an appreciation and respect for diversity
5. To provide students with the opportunity to develop cross-cultural awareness and sensitivity

Activities Before Reading

- Show your students the cover of the book, and ask them to name the two animals on the cover, bats and birds. Then ask them to name what similarities the animals seem to have. They might say that both can fly, both are tan in color (on the cover), both have wings, both have feet, and both have eyes and a mouth. Ask them if they know any differences between the two animals. They might answer that birds have feathers while bats are furry, bats have ears but birds do not, and bats are nocturnal while birds fly in the daytime.
- Tell them to think about their own families as they listen to this story and to think about how they are similar in many ways to their brothers and sisters, but are still unique and individual in other ways.

Activities After Reading

- Once you have finished the book, ask your students to reflect on how Stellaluna was a little bit like her adopted bird family. Students might answer that she lived with them in a nest, she ate their food, and she flew with them during the day. Then ask how she was different. Here they might mention how she slept upside down, how she hated to eat bugs, and couldn't land on a branch like the birds. Point out that she held on to some of her bat ways and still slept upside down. Invite your students to share examples of how they have held on to aspects of their own culture while adapting to other cultures.
- Ask your students to think of the ways in which they are similar to their own family members, and yet have individual traits. They may answer that they look like their siblings, but have different colored hair, or eyes, or skin tone. Then have them look around the class and notice the

similarities and differences that exist. Chart their ideas on the board by making two categories: "Share" and "Individual." Under the "Share" category they may say that they are all human beings, they all attend the same school, and they are all in the same grade. Under "Individual" they may list physical traits only, so encourage them to add cultural traits, such as nationalities, favorite foods, languages spoken, games played, greeting used, and so on. Then look at the chart and talk with your students about the beauty of being an individual—that even when you belong to a group, you are special and unique. Many of our unique attributes can be directly traced to our cultural experiences and the places where we have lived.

• Why was the bird's mother upset when she saw the baby birds hanging upside down? It is possible that she was afraid because it was different. She also may have thought it was dangerous for her children. Explain that sometimes people are afraid of ways that are different from their own, especially if they don't understand them. Explore ways people can learn about differences to increase their understanding.

• The lifestyles of bats vary widely. Using the "bat notes" at the end of the book, identify the ways they are different. They look different, have different behaviors, eat different foods, live in different climates, and use different physical characteristics to find their way. The lifestyles of people vary in similar ways. Ask your students to compare their lifestyles to those of another culture they have known.

• Have your students complete a "web" to identify the cultural influences on their lives. Ask them to put their names in the center and connect circles to show each person or place that has had an influence on them and in what way. Have your students draw self-portraits reflecting one or more of those influences. For example, a child might draw a picture of himself with a baseball bat in front of Big Ben.

Transition Education Links

This story has links with objectives in Chapter 3, "The Process of Transition." Stellaluna feels embarrassed when she cannot fly and land like the birds. Ask your students to think about a time when they were embarrassed because their behavior was different from the people in the culture they were in. This could have been something that happened to them when they moved to another country or to their current home. Explain that this is natural for anyone living in or visiting a culture different from their own. Encourage your students to have a sense of humor about their mistakes and know that if they give themselves time and observe the different ways of doing things, they will learn to adapt too. Explain that this is all part of the process of transition.

Explore the experience of cultural adaptation. Write the word *adapt* on the board and ask your students to define it. According to Webster's dictionary, *to adapt* means "to adjust oneself to a different environment." Ask your students to list the ways that Stellaluna had to adapt while living with the birds. (She ate bugs instead of fruit, flew by day instead of night, and hung by her thumbs instead of her feet.) Invite them to share ways they have had to adapt to the place they are living now.

Explain that whenever we move to a new culture we adapt to living in a different environment. Ask for volunteers to share how things in the school or community where they are living now are different from where they lived before. This will give everyone in the class an opportunity to learn things about each other's cultures. Begin modeling this yourself by giving an example: "When I lived in Brazil, school summer holidays always started in December. But here, our summer holiday starts in June."

When we experience different cultures, we learn to adapt our behavior to fit the situation. In the same way, the birds adapted to being with the bats and hung upside down. When they returned to their nest, they probably behaved as birds again. Discuss situations where your students adapt their behavior depending on the culture they are in. An example might be, when they visit their Japanese friend, they take their shoes off when they enter the house, and when they visit their American friend, they keep them on. Acknowledge that we may also change our behavior to fit different situations within the same culture. This adaptability shows an awareness and sensitivity to other cultures.

This story also has links to Chapter 5, "Friendships and Relationships" because of the unique friendship that Stellaluna had with the baby birds. If a friend is someone who accepts you just as you are, then ask the class if the baby birds accepted Stellaluna. (Yes, they did in spite of her differences.) Now ask your students to think of a good friend who is different from them. This person may be of a different nationality, religion, or race. Then have the students list the traits that they admire in that friend, and as a class compose a "Friendship" chart, listing traits that can help you be a friend to someone else.

At the end of the story the birds question, "How can we be so different and feel so much alike? And how can we feel so different and be so much alike?" "I think it's quite a mystery," Flap chirped. Stellaluna then responds, "I agree. But we're friends. And that's a fact." Use this dialogue to discuss the similarities and differences that exist in friendships, and invite your students to share examples from their own lives.

LESSON PLAN, GRADES K–5

Grandfather's Journey
by Allen Say

Synopsis

This biographical picture book tells the story of how, as a young man, Allen Say's grandfather left his native country of Japan to travel throughout the United States. His grandfather eventually returns to Japan to marry, and brings his Japanese bride back to California to live. In time, the grandfather misses his homeland so much that he and his wife decide to return to Japan to live. However, the grandfather misses much of what life was like in California and begins to dream of one day returning again. In time, the grandfather's daughter marries a man she has met in Japan, and they later have a son, who grows up hearing his grandfather's stories of California. When the son becomes a young man, he decides to move there. He then understands why his grandfather was always torn between his Japanese homeland and his adopted California home, and the love he had for both places.

Objectives

1. To provide students with the opportunity to gain an understanding of what culture is and how it is learned
2. To provide students with the opportunity to explore their cultural identity
3. To provide students with the opportunity to share their cultural backgrounds with others
4. To provide students with the opportunity to develop an appreciation and respect for cultural diversity

Activities Before Reading

• Ask your students to tell you the names of the countries where they have lived. Students who have not moved abroad can still share the names of places they have lived. Compile a list of the country names on chart paper. Place a self-adhesive colored dot next to each country or state for every child who has lived there to create a graph showing the number of children who have lived in each place. Have the children interpret the data and rank the countries and states according to the number of dots from highest to lowest. Children will be interested in the different countries and states their classmates have lived in and may find that they have had common experiences. Identify the location of each country by placing a self-adhesive dot on a world map. Talk about how living in other countries gives us unique experiences and perspectives on our own culture.

Activities After Reading

- List and discuss the different experiences that the grandfather had while traveling in the United States. (He was impressed with the vastness of the country, the factories, the natural beauty, the scale, the different types of transportation, and the diversity of the people.) The experience of travel made an impact on him and inspired him to want to travel more. Provide an opportunity for your students to share their travel experiences that have inspired them. Let them know that because of their travels and experiences, they too may long to explore more of the world.

- Discuss the two cultures of Japan and the United States with your class. What did grandfather enjoy about each place? Ask them why we adopt different aspects of the cultures where we live, and in what ways do we learn our own native culture from our parents? Why was it that the grandfather could not just be happy with one of the cultures? (He was a part of both cultures and had learned to appreciate different aspects of each culture.) Point out that it is often through experiencing another culture that our awareness and appreciation of our own culture is heightened.

- Now revisit the wall map, and ask for volunteers to name one aspect of a culture they have lived in other than their home culture that they have incorporated into their lives as a result of having lived abroad. For example, one student may say that he loves to eat cheese fondue as a result of having lived in Switzerland for a year. Another student may say that she likes wearing the pair of clogs she bought while living in Sweden. Follow up each example with a counterpart from their own culture. For example, ask the student who loves fondue, what favorite food he has from his own culture. Gather as many examples as possible and write them on the board in pairs. Then continue with the discussion showing your students that as people live within other cultures they adopt new ideas, while retaining their own unique cultural identity as well.

- Refer back to the page in the book where the grandfather had met many different types of men in America. The illustration shows six men from different ethnic backgrounds standing in front of a barbershop (p. 12). The world itself is becoming more mobile with people of many different cultures living outside of their home countries. Discuss the benefits of how much richer our lives are because of all the different people we have met and learned from. Ask the children if they have examples of people whose different cultures have enriched their own lives with new experiences and understanding.

Suggested Follow-up Activities

   • Using the first two pages from the book as an example, encourage students to compile a personal cultural journal of their own lives. The first page should be a title page. Then continuing with the journal, on the left page the students are to draw a picture of the type of clothing popular in their passport country, or home culture. On the right page they should draw clothes that are popular in another culture, where they are living now or have lived at one time. The journal should continue in the same format where the left page depicts aspects of their own culture and the right page shows corresponding cultural aspects of the other home and lifestyle. Encourage students to include the landscape, homes, and pastimes, and the deeper aspects of culture such as greetings, celebrations, and traditions. Invite students to share their completed journals with their peers.
   • As a child, Allen loved hearing his grandfather's stories about California. If possible, have your students ask their grandparents to tape one of their favorite stories or a favorite memory from their childhood that they share with their grandchild. Alternatively, parents can share a favorite family story or memory. Have the children play their tapes as a way of sharing their family culture. Explain that through shared stories, family histories and traditions are passed down from one generation to the next.
   • Have the children create books that represent their cultural backgrounds or places that have been a part of their lives. They can include sketches of people, watercolor paintings of scenes of special places, poetry, or phrases that evoke a sense of place. Celebrate the sharing of these books with each other.

Transition Education Links

   This story can be linked with objectives in Chapter 2, "The Common Experience of Mobility." In this story both the grandfather and author felt a yearning for both places and saw both Japan and California as "home." Explain that this may happen to some of you or people you know. Explore the concept of "home" with your students and provide the opportunity for them to explore where "home" is for them. It may be more than one place as well.

   This story also has links to Chapter 7, "Moving Back." Even though the grandfather found his old home to be the same, he himself was different. Discuss the idea that nothing stays the same. Ask, "While the grandfather was delighted that he had moved back to Japan, do you think he anticipated his longing for California?" Use that section of the story to talk about the expectations and reality of moving back home to a country after you have been gone for a while. Help your students establish what their hopes would be in terms of their expectations for moving back, and what realities might exist.

LESSON PLAN, GRADES K–5

When I Was Young in the Mountains
by Cynthia Rylant

Synopsis

The author reminisces about her childhood growing up in the Appalachian Mountains in the United States. She shares her special memories that evoke a strong sense of place, family, and way of life. This story lends itself beautifully to opportunities for children to celebrate their own childhoods and cultural backgrounds, and learn more about their classmates.

Objectives

1. To provide students with the opportunity to explore the cultural influences in their lives
2. To provide students with the opportunity to gain a greater sense of self-awareness and understanding of their own cultural identities
3. To provide students with the opportunity to share their cultural backgrounds and the knowledge of other cultures or places they have experienced
4. To provide students with the opportunity to learn more about each other and develop an appreciation and respect for cultural diversity

Activities Before Reading

• Share your own background with your students. Invite students to share the place they were born, how long they lived there, any other countries or states they have lived in, and which one they remember or know best. Have each student share with a partner a special memory that comes to mind from that place.

• Introduce the story *When I Was Young in the Mountains* by Cynthia Rylant. Ask for predictions based on the title and cover. Ask, "What do you think the author is trying to convey in this book?"

Activities After Reading

• Invite the students' personal responses. Ask, "How did you feel as I read the story? What were you thinking as you listened to the author's words and looked at the illustrations? Did they trigger any memories of your own? What did the author do to convey the richness of her memories?"

• Introduce the project of writing and publishing their own books based on this one, such as *When I was Young in Brazil, When I was Young in Japan,* or *When I was Young in Holland.* Young children can write books such as *I am Young in . . .* , which will likely be a treasure in later years! Encourage your students to think about the people, places, feelings, and events they remember that are particularly special to them. Have them consider the aspects of culture that have been an important part of their lives as well as the cultural influences of significant people in their lives, such as a Honduran au pair, Swedish grandfather, or German teacher. Nonmobile children can create books that capture their childhood memories, and include any cultural influences in their lives.

Adapt the activity for children who have lived in several places. Their book may be entitled *When I was Young in Spain and Canada,* or they may write a double book, *When I Was Young in . . .* on the left pages and *I Am Older In . . .* on the right, to capture both the past and present.

Encourage the students to use their senses when thinking about their special memories. Are there sights, smells, or sounds that they particularly remember? Encourage students to take a small detail—a thought, memory, or idea—and grow it into something bigger.

Have students use the writing process to develop their stories. Plan illustrations and make books. The published books can be shared as part of a celebration of the diverse backgrounds represented in the class and link with many other areas of the curriculum.

Suggested Follow-up Activities

• Have your students create a photo collage of their childhoods depicting the different places and cultural influences in their lives.
• Have students create self-portrait puppets that reflect their cultural selves.

Transition Education Links

This story links with objectives in Chapter 2, "The Common Experience of Mobility." It provides children with the opportunity to reflect on and share special memories of the place or places where they grew up.

LESSON PLAN, GRADES K–5

little blue and little yellow
by Leo Lionni

Synopsis

Little blue has many friends of different colors, but his best friend is little yellow. They play together and sit next to each other in school. One day they hug each other until they become green, and their parents no longer recognize them. Little blue and little yellow cry until they turn back to their original colors. However, their parents soon realize what had happened, and they all happily turn a little green. This story illustrates the concept that cultural differences in our friendships and relationships can influence and enrich our lives.

Objectives

1. To provide students with the opportunity to gain an understanding of what culture is and how it is learned
2. To provide students with the opportunity to explore the cultural influences in their lives
3. To provide students with the opportunity to gain a greater sense of self-awareness and understanding of their own cultural identity
4. To provide students with the opportunity to gain an appreciation of their cultural or multicultural selves

Activities Before Reading

• Ask your school librarian to help you collect books with photographs of children and adults from other cultures. Your school may have a picture file showing food, clothing, artifacts, music, dance, buildings, handicrafts, or celebrations from different cultures that can also be used. Children can also bring items from home or from their neighbors. Use these as a springboard to discuss culture. What is culture? What aspects of culture do you see in these photographs? Establish that culture is a shared way of life that includes objects and customs as well as the values and beliefs we hold.

 • Ask your students to think of the cultures in their families and share them with the class. What are they and how are they reflected in their lives? Is it the food they eat, the clothes they wear, the celebrations they have, or the traditions they follow?

 • Ask them to think about a time they participated in the cultural celebrations of friends or neighbors, or a time they shared their celebrations with others. What were they and what did they learn and enjoy? Explain that in this story the colors represent our cultural selves. It shows how two friends can share in each other's culture and have it become a part of who they are.

Activities After Reading

 • Using overhead transparencies of one blue circle and one yellow circle, demonstrate the influence of culture on the two friends by overlapping the colors on an overhead projector. Ask your students to think about a friend whose culture is different from their own and who has influenced their life in some way. What are some of the things they have gained that are now a part of their life? For example, they may now have a love of Indian curries after sharing meals with an Indian friend, or they may enjoy playing bocci, which they learned from an Italian friend, or making origami, which their Japanese friend had taught them. Emphasize that when the characters in the story turned a little green, they were enriched by the culture of their friend yet they maintained their own cultural identity.

 • Discuss the reasons their parents might not have recognized the two friends. Explain that sometimes children have different experiences than their parents and may adopt different cultural practices or develop a different cultural awareness. Sometimes children can teach their parents about appreciating and valuing differences.

 • Have the children complete a Venn diagram to represent the sharing of culture between themselves and a friend. Alternatively, this activity can be used to illustrate the cultural influences from different places a child has lived or the different cultures of their parents to reflect their multicultural identity. As children see the diversity in their backgrounds, they can gain a greater appreciation of the diversity in the lives of others and in our world.

 • Provide opportunities for your students to share aspects of their family culture or cultures with the class. This can be through a Cultural Sharing Day where children bring a snack or music to share, teach the class how to do an art project, or read a poem or story that reflects their cultural background. You and your class can add your own ideas!

Suggested Follow-up Activities

• Celebrate an International Day in your class or school community. Ask the children and their families to bring a dish from their cultural background to share. Include music and dance. Encourage the children to dress in a way that reflects their cultural or multicultural selves. For example, for a child from Ghana and the United States, African kente cloth and a baseball cap may be most authentic!

• Plan an International Games Day where students teach each other a game that is popular in their family or country.

Transition Education Links

This story links with objectives in Chapter 3, "The Process of Transition." Discuss the process of transition, and explain that through the process of adapting to another culture we all "change color" a bit as we are influenced by the cross-cultural experiences we have.

This story has links with objectives in Chapter 5, "Friendships and Relationships" as children can further explore the ways the cultural differences in their friendships enrich their lives. Discuss the things they have learned and enjoyed as a result of these relationships, as well as the things they have taught others about their cultural heritage.

LESSON PLAN, GRADES 4–5

Seedfolks
by Paul Fleischman

Synopsis

This story involves 13 different characters that come into each other's lives because of a vacant lot in an inner city section of Cleveland, Ohio, where they all live. At first the lot is vacant, but then it slowly becomes transformed as each of the characters come together to help fashion it into a garden. Just as the lot becomes transformed, so do the characters as they begin to touch each other's lives. The characters are diverse in their personalities, nationalities, and cultural backgrounds, yet they each find personal meaning through the garden, and a way to connect with others. (One of the characters is a young Mexican teenage girl who is pregnant. If this subject would be inappropriate for your students, then do not read the chapter titled "Maricela.")

Objectives

1. To provide students with the opportunity to gain a greater sense of self-awareness and understanding of their own cultural identity
2. To provide students with the opportunity to develop an appreciation and respect for cultural diversity
3. To provide students with the opportunity to develop cross-cultural awareness and sensitivity

Activities Before Reading

• Ask your class to close their eyes and picture a garden in their mind. Tell them to concentrate on what plants are growing in that garden and see the colors, the heights, and the array of all the plants in this garden. Ask them to open their eyes and write down words describing the visual images they saw or do a quick sketch. Have your students share aloud what type of garden they were imagining. Chart their responses on the board. Go over all of the ideas to see how varied the responses were. Point out that no two people saw the garden in the exact same way, that each person's ideas were unique; yet when the ideas were put together, they formed a complete and richly varied picture. Extend that thought to a classroom community, how each individual student is unique, but together the class makes a diverse whole, just like the garden they imagined. Discuss how in the same way unique individuals join together to form a neighborhood, country, and world community. Tell the students you are going to read aloud a story in which 12 or 13 characters who do not know each other at the beginning of the story come together to form a special garden.

Activities After Reading

• List each of the characters from the story on the board so students will be able to remember how each character was unique and had a story to tell.

Kim (Vietnamese)	Ana (Rumanian)
Wendall (American)	Gonzalo (Guatemalan)
Leona (African American)	Sam (Jewish)
Virgil (Haitian)	Sae Young (Korean)

around an almond" (p. 61). "I wonder if others knew as little about Indians as I had known about Poles" (pp. 63–64).

Invite your students to describe a time they were open-minded about learning about another person and his or her cultural background, or a time someone showed interest in learning about theirs. In what ways was it a positive experience for everyone?

Ask your students to choose a character's story that speaks to them and lead a discussion about it or respond to it in their journal. Encourage them to find a particular quote that is meaningful to them. Some examples or suggestions are: "This time she gave me a little smile. I smiled back" (p. 24). "Feel very glad inside. Feel part of garden. Almost like family" (p. 39).

Suggested Follow-up Activities

• Create a "cultural garden" in your classroom. You can do this by designating a place in the room, defined perhaps by a large piece of mural paper, as your "vacant lot." Ask each student to bring in something from home that represents his or her own ethnic background, and have each student place that item on the "lot." Once all the items have been displayed, give the students an opportunity to share why they chose their particular item and ask how it represents their cultural background.

• If possible at your school, create an actual garden and grow flowers, herbs, fruits, or vegetables from the countries represented in your class. Enjoy sharing these within the school community.

• Host a Harvest Festival or International Feast to celebrate the cultural diversity in your class and school community. Have students bring in food from their countries or those that reflect their cultural backgrounds to share with each other and invited guests.

• This book provides an opportunity to address the particular transition issues facing immigrant and refugee children and their families. Like Gonzalo, some children may have a better command of the language in the new country and have the additional responsibilities of interpreting the language or communicating with members of the community for their family. What other situations or problems might they face? Invite your immigrant and refugee students to share their own experiences. Gonzalo's story is quite poignant as he recognizes the difficulties facing members of his family as they experience a loss of place within the new community.

Transition Education Links

This book has links with Chapter 5, "Friendships and Relationships." The characters in the stories meet through their shared interest in garden-

Curtis (African American)   Nora (British)
Maricela (Mexican)   Amir (Indian)
Florence (African American)

Ask how the story might have been different if all the characters ha(
the same nationality: Would the individual stories have been so diffe
In what ways do the characters themselves represent the garden? (Ea
them had a different story to tell, but together they were connected b
garden and the desire to help it flourish and grow. Through the gai
they were able to express an important part of themselves and keep t
memories alive.)

- Now link this to your own class. How are your students uniq
(They may come from many different backgrounds and have had dif
ent life experiences.) What binds your students together? (Your class a
community of learners.) How can your class be compared to a gard(
(Each student is an individual with his or her own personal and cultu
identity, but together the students make up the cohesive unit of a cla$

- Each character had his or her own point of view about the vaca
lot and the ensuing garden. In the beginning most of the characters did n
really know each other and in some instances were distrustful of each othe
However, by the end of the story they worked together to create and su
tain the garden. Ask your class to relate this to school. Why is it importal
for everyone to get along and work together, regardless of their differences
(This makes for a stronger community, and we can learn from the cultura
differences of others to enhance our knowledge of the world.)

- Now make the point that each of us (including the teacher) has a
cultural identity and that cultural identity shapes our perspective of the
world and the way we have experienced it. Discuss the reasons people are
generally more comfortable around other people of their same background.
(They have more in common with those people, and similar backgrounds
represent what is known. Usually, too, they are familiar with the language,
customs, and ways of thinking of others who share their same cultural
background.) Discuss ways we can approach cultural differences so that
we can understand them better. Ask your students to describe a time they
had to adjust to a new cultural situation. Did they ask questions, observe
the differences, show an interest in others, or try to adapt their behavior?
Explore the cross-cultural skills they used that were helpful.

- Amir's story illustrates the importance of getting to know people
as individuals and refraining from stereotyping others. Discuss the message in this story and the important lessons Amir learned using the following quotes: "When I heard her words, I realized how useless was all
that I'd heard about Poles, how much richness it hid, like the worthless shell

ing and through caring for the garden they have created. Invite your students to describe a time they met someone new by discovering shared interests. Have these relationships included children from other cultures?

This book also links with Chapter 6, "Problem-Solving Skills." The characters in each story had some sort of problem in their lives, and once they became involved with the garden, their lives took on a new focus. All the characters were faced with the same decision—to become involved with the garden or to remain isolated. For each chapter and each character, have your students identify what the problem seemed to be, and how the vacant-lot-turned-garden provided a solution. Invite your students to describe problems they have encountered and ways they have solved them.

IDEAS FOR CROSS-CURRICULAR CONNECTIONS

Creative and Performing Arts

Provide your students with an opportunity to explore the art associated with different cultures. Find out how many different cultures are represented in your classroom, and then with your students research the artwork that is representative of those cultures. Perhaps a few of your students' parents could come in and share some artwork from their country as well. There are some very definitive types of art for certain cultures, like the iconoclastic art of Russia, the woven textile art of Scandinavia, and the brush painting of Japan. Exposing your students to different types of art helps foster a sense of pride in their own cultural heritage and expands their knowledge about the cultures of their classmates.

Have the children research artists or composers from the countries represented in your class. Celebrate the contributions these individuals have made. Have the children create art inspired by one of the artists. It might include a study of Picasso, Chagall, or Monet. You might enlist the help of your art teacher.

Invite parents to demonstrate musical instruments or teach native dancing from the countries of children in your class.

Social Studies

While it is said that all history can be told by starting "once upon a time," geography can be studied by starting "once upon a place." As you help your students understand their own personal and cultural identities, you can also highlight the study of geography in terms of culture. For example, pick out mountainous regions of the world and look at how those mountains affected both the history and the culture of the people who lived there. In the same way you can study the great deserts of the world and see how the culture of the native people was shaped by the geography of the land. Even something as simple as how clothing is designed to meet the climactic conditions can become a cultural influence. Think of how people in hot desert areas dress in loose fitting garments that we now associate with their culture. Look at the effect of geography and climate on different types of homes, occupations, crops produced, and industries. Have each child consider the impact of geography on their particular culture. How is it reflected in the art and music of the people?

Teach landforms through the countries of the students represented in your class. For example, when you study rivers, an Egyptian student might research the Nile, an Italian student might choose the Tiber, and an American student might learn about the Mississippi River. The children can share their knowledge of other places they have lived or visited. Consider having the children use what they know about a place to write a fictional piece, such as "Life on the Tiber River," pretending they or characters they develop are living there.

Science

Have your students research a scientist from their home country or another country where they have lived. Help develop an appreciation of diversity by celebrating the contributions from individuals from many countries or places around the world.

Math

Use the different systems of measurements to link with cultural identity. In many parts of the world the metric system is used for measurement, while in other parts of the world the imperial system is employed. All of us identify with the system we were taught originally and learning a new system is often confusing. Help your students by teaching both systems and also calling attention to which system is used in which parts of the world. That way, a student who has seen his parents buy a kilogram of cheese at the market will be able to identify a part of his or her culture through scientific measurement.

Food perhaps more than any other item helps us to define our cultural identity. Instead of hosting an international meal where students bring in different foods from their cultures, host an international recipe day where students bring in a recipe from home that is from their culture. Reproduce the recipes and use them as a math lesson to teach measurement, fractions, addition, and so on. This lesson would be a good follow-up to the lesson above on the metric system since some of the recipes most likely will use metric measurements. As a culminating activity, actually follow some of the recipes and prepare the dishes to share!

Chapter 5

Friendships and Relationships

Humans are social beings. We all want friends and we all need friends in our lives. Friendships can bring us tremendous joy and comfort, and contribute to a full and satisfying life. Without them our world would be quite lonely indeed. It is therefore not surprising that leaving and making friends are among the greatest concerns for both adults *and* children who move.

Learning how to make and keep friends are some of the most important life skills one can acquire. While effective interpersonal skills are important for everyone, they are particularly essential for children who move and have to establish new relationships. Children who move frequently are continually meeting new people, and their relationships are constantly changing.

These skills do not always come naturally to children and need to be both taught and practiced. While some children will have developed strong interpersonal skills from parents, family members, teachers, or other influential people in their lives, other children may have had few positive role models. It is therefore important to provide your students with multiple learning opportunities to develop these skills that are integrated throughout your entire program.

Some children who move are quite adaptable and look forward to the opportunity to meet new people and make new friends. They form new friendships easily while others may have difficulty. While you cannot force friendships, you can help facilitate relationships between your students by assigning buddies or pairing students for project work. Children who do not speak the same language can work together on art or music activities. We encourage you to look for ways to facilitate friendships that do not rely on language.

For many children who move, particularly those who move frequently, making friends becomes quite difficult. They may be reluctant to get close to others as it is very painful when they move away. It is important to help children see the value of friendship and appreciate the pleasure and richness that having friends can bring to their lives, even if it is for a short time. Sometimes some of the best friendships we have are with those we have known for the shortest time. Encourage children to take risks to approach new children wherever they may live, and for however long it may be.

Be aware that some children who move are desperate to find a "best friend," and focus on one person and exclude the possibility of relationships with any others. Help your students see that they can be friends with more than one person, and that friends can be shared.

CONCEPTS FEATURED IN ACTIVITIES

1. *Similarities and differences exist between all people*. Similarities and differences exist between people in a wide range of areas. They include physical characteristics, abilities, interests, hobbies, cultural practices, languages spoken, and many more. As you explore these with your students, help them recognize the human characteristics we all have in common and value and respect our differences. Help your students learn about similarities and differences between people by beginning with members in their own families and their friends and classmates.

2. *There are many different kinds of relationships*. Throughout our lives we have many different types of relationships. We develop relationships with family members, friends, teachers, neighbors, colleagues, and even pets. We form friendships with some people, while others remain acquaintances or people we interact with in our neighborhood. Explore the concept of friendship with your students and provide opportunities to discuss questions such as, "What is a friend?" "What qualities make a good friend?" Explore the different levels of closeness that can exist in friendships. It is important for children to be aware of the different kinds of relationships that can exist and the satisfaction each can bring.

3. *Effective skills in establishing and maintaining friendships can be developed*. All children benefit by developing effective ways to establish and maintain friendships with other children. Provide ongoing opportunities for your students to learn ways to make new friends, be a friend, and keep friends, and to put them into practice. Give particular attention to how these skills can be used anywhere, especially when moving to a new place. Children can learn to listen, share, cooperate, solve problems, and develop empathy for others.

4. *Cultural differences can exist in friendships*. Friends can be different in many ways. In particular, children can develop meaningful friendships with children of different cultural backgrounds. They can find ways to share

and have fun with each other even though they may practice different customs or have different ways of communicating or expressing themselves. Through friendship children are able to understand and appreciate cultural differences, and learn to adapt to different cultural situations.

5. *Cultural differences can influence and enrich our lives.* Children benefit from friendships with children of other cultures in many ways. They learn new ways of doing things, try different foods, share in each other's celebrations, learn each other's language, play each other's games, and listen to each other's music. Some of these new experiences may even become part of their daily lives.

6. *Friendships can continue after someone moves away.* We know that it is very difficult for children when a friend moves away, both for the friend who is leaving and the one who is staying behind. Unfortunately, even with the best of intentions, people get involved in their new lives and old friendships can fall away. This is often very painful for children when a friendship has been particularly meaningful in their lives. Children need support in finding ways to stay in touch with their friends once they or their friend has moved. Provide opportunities for your students to explore ways to stay in touch. These may include sending E-mail; writing letters; sending photographs, poems, stories, or drawings; or creating a Web site. You and your students can brainstorm other ideas. Encourage parents to support their children's efforts to stay in touch with their friends as well.

7. *Mobility can affect our friendships in significant ways.* With each move, children are faced with making new friends. For some, this is an exciting opportunity to meet new people; for others, it is a daunting experience. Some children are reluctant to reach out to others yet again as it is too painful when one or the other eventually leaves. Others have a sense of urgency and can come on quite strong. Help children become aware of their responses and the ways they make new friends when they move. It is important to encourage children to allow time for new relationships to develop.

8. *People can develop empathy for the feelings of those who are moving away, staying behind, or arriving in a new community.* If they have not moved themselves, most children know someone who has moved whether it is a friend, neighbor, or relative. As children learn more about what the experience of moving is like, they can develop empathy for those who are moving, staying behind, or arriving in the community. Help them explore ways they can reach out to others and take the initiative in welcoming new classmates to the school community. Discuss ways they can be sensitive to the needs of children who are moving away or who are losing a good friend. Help

children to see that each one of us can make a difference in another person's life.

Objectives: To provide students with the opportunity

- to learn about the ways people are alike and different
- to explore the nature of friendships and relationships
- to develop effective skills to establish and maintain friendships
- to explore the cultural differences that can exist in friendships
- to explore the ways cultural differences can influence and enrich friendships
- to identify ways to continue friendships after someone has moved away
- to learn about the ways that mobility can affect our relationships
- to develop empathy for those who are moving away, staying behind, or arriving in a new community, and explore ways to reach out and support them

LESSON PLAN, GRADES K–5

Best Friends Together Again
by Aliki

Synopsis

This book is the delightful sequel to *We Are Best Friends* highlighted in Chapter 3. In this story, Robert and Peter are reunited when Peter comes to visit for 2 weeks. Robert wonders if Peter will still be the same and if he will still like him. Both boys find that, while some things may have changed, their friendship still remains strong.

Objectives

1. To provide students with the opportunity to see that friendships can continue after someone has moved away
2. To provide students with the opportunity to explore the different kinds of relationships that exist
3. To provide students with the opportunity to learn about the ways mobility can affect our relationships
4. To provide students with the opportunity to develop effective skills to maintain friendships

Activities Before Reading

• Ask your students to think about a friendship they have with someone who lives in another place. How has the friendship continued since they or the person moved away? Have your students share the ways they keep up with their friends from other places and chart those ideas. Brainstorm additional ways to keep close when you live far apart from someone you care about. Although it is not the same as living nearby, how can you can keep close and really share in each other's lives?

• Tell them there are several things we can learn about friendship from this story. Ask them to think about what they are as you read to them.

Activities After Reading

• Ask your students what they noticed about the ways the characters in the story each displayed the qualities of being a good friend.

It is important for children to learn that they can be good friends with more than one person at a time. Explain that children who move often feel a strong need to have one best friend and it is helpful for them to see that friends can be shared. Discuss the ways Robert and Peter shared their friends. While both boys had fun and shared activities with their new friends, they still remained good friends with each other. They enjoyed time alone together and also played with the other children. Both boys were open about their new friends and didn't get jealous of the other person. Although Peter was unsure about meeting Will, he did it anyway and was friendly toward him. Will was friendly as well. The boys all played together with their other friends, and weren't possessive of each other.

• Robert was worried about whether Peter would be the same and whether he would still like him. These are natural worries for people who have not seen each other in a while. Discuss some of the worries your students have had before meeting up with an old friend. These may include whether they will still like the same things and have fun together. Explain that sometimes old friends do grow apart, but with effort on both parts they can stay in touch and continue to create new memories.

• Chart together the things that stayed the same (Robert's toy chest, his puppets, blocks, and cars; they still liked the same sandwiches) and those that were different (Both had gotten bigger; the way Robert's room was arranged; his new pet gerbil; a new lamp; and more books). Point out that when friends are apart, life goes on and some things change, but some things do stay the same; and if there is a good friendship, it can continue.

• When Robert and Peter got together, they built a fort like old times, had their favorite sandwiches for lunch, and reminisced about old times. What would you do if you could get together with an old friend?

• Peter learned to make paper airplanes from his new friend Alex. He then taught Robert, Will, and the other children how to make them too. Ask your students, "What is something you could teach a new friend? Is there something new you have learned that you could share with an old friend?" Have your students draw names, and ask each child to choose something to teach to his or her partner. Help them plan how and what they will do. It could be making an art project, preparing a recipe, or learning a new game or song. Celebrate a Friendship Sharing Day.

Suggested Follow-up Activities

• Have your students write an acrostic poem about an old friend who has moved away. They can include pictures or photographs and mail them to their friend. Here is one Robert could have written for Peter.

PETER
Paper airplane maker
Eats peanut butter and jelly sandwiches
Thinks up good names
Everlasting friend
Remembers the fun times we've had

• Have your students make an audiotape to send to a friend who lives in another place. Discuss ways to make the message meaningful such as sharing about things they have in common, asking them about what they have been doing too, and remembering things that were special to both of them.

Transition Education Links

This story has links with objectives in Chapter 3, "The Process of Transition." One thing that can help ease the process of transition is knowing we can still maintain friendships with our special friends after we or they move away. This story illustrates the way that two friends have done just that. Help your students plan ways to keep in touch with friends they are leaving.

It also links with objectives in Chapter 6, "Problem-Solving Skills." Discuss ways to be inclusive of both old and new friends. The children in the story had clear communication and asked about the other's new friend. Have your students role-play a telephone conversation between two friends who show genuine interest in each other's life.

LESSON PLAN, GRADES K–5

Mrs. Katz and Tush
by Patricia Polacco

Synopsis

Mrs. Katz is an elderly Polish widow whom Larnel and his mother visit daily. Even though Larnel's family and Mrs. Katz are from two different cultures, their friendship is strong through the common bonds they share. Larnel gives Mrs. Katz a kitten whom she names Tush; and when Tush disappears one night, the entire community becomes involved looking for her. By the end of the story the two families have become more than just friends, they have become a deep part of each other's lives.

Objectives

1. To provide students with the opportunity to learn about the ways people are alike and different
2. To provide students with the opportunity to explore the nature of friendships and relationships
3. To provide students with the opportunity to develop effective skills to establish friendships
4. To provide students with the opportunity to explore the ways cultural differences can influence and enrich friendships

Activities Before Reading

• Ask your students if they have ever known a person in their community whose culture was different from their own. How did their family get to know this person? What was it about this person's culture that was interesting, or made them an interesting person? Give students a piece of paper and ask them to do a "bio-sketch," where you simply list details about another person that give clues about who they are in terms of culture. We encourage you to model an example of a bio-sketch from your own life. An example might be:

Mrs. "B"
neighbor down the street
Greek
wonderful baker of Greek cookies

jet black hair
different selection of artifacts (artwork, collectibles)
goes to a different type of church than my family
listens to different music than I do

• Then tell your students to hold onto their bio-sketches while you read the following story about a young African American boy and the older Polish neighbor who became his friend

Activities After Reading

• After reading this story, ask your class to note the differences that existed between Larnel and Mrs. Katz. (They were of different ages, different nationalities, different sexes, different religions, and different ethnicities.) Now ask them to note what things they shared in common that helped their relationship turn into a friendship. (They both loved Tush; they enjoyed having an afternoon snack together that Mrs. Katz baked and Larnel relished; they had both experienced prejudice; and they both respected each other's differences.) Point out that even though we may be different from our classmates, we all share many similarities regardless of which culture is our home culture.

• Put the two words *relationship* and *friendship* on the board, and ask your class to differentiate between the two. Ask your students, "Can a friendship also be a relationship? Can a relationship also be a friendship? How does a relationship blossom into a friendship?" In this story, Mrs. Katz and Larnel first get acquainted because they are neighbors and Larnel's mother goes to check in on Mrs. Katz after Mrs. Katz's husband has died. Ask your students at which point in the story the relationship begins to blossom into a friendship and what the catalyst was for that change. (It really begins with Tush, when Larnel senses the older woman's loneliness and brings her the kitten as a gift. However, it is his agreement to come and help take care of Tush that really launches the friendship and gives them the opportunity of visiting with each other on a daily basis.) Tell them the old axiom, "In order to have a friend, you must first be a friend," and ask them what they think that means. In what way did Larnel reach out to Mrs. Katz first? (He brought her the kitten to help keep her company.)

• Ask your students to refer back to their bio-sketches and see if they can remember an event or catalyst that started to make the person in their bio-sketch more a friend than an acquaintance. Going back to the model suggested at the beginning of this lesson, you could add, "She came to our house one Christmas with her special homemade Greek cookies as a gift." The important thing is for students to recognize that friendships do not just happen by chance. There is almost always an instance of one person reaching out to the other that makes the relationship move on to a higher level. Have them add a catalyst to their own bio-sketch.

• Now have your students take their bio-sketches and incorporate them into a short narrative. They may entitle it "The Mrs. Katz in My Life" or something to that effect. Tell them to include all the details from the bio-sketch, but to expand upon that sketch by including where this person lived, who they were, how your family met them, the interactions you had, and so on. Once students have finished and polished the writing, give them an opportunity to share their narratives aloud.

Suggested Follow-up Activities

• One very poignant part in this story is when Mrs. Katz takes Larnel to the cemetery and they each place a small rock on Mr. Katz's headstone. Although Larnel is not Jewish, he respects Mrs. Katz's religious beliefs because they are important to her. Ask your students to think of a friend they have now, or have had in the past, whose culture or religion is different from their own. Then ask them to think of one aspect of that friend's culture or religion that they recognize as being different from their own life but an aspect that they respect in the friend's life. It might be as simple as a different type of food served at a holiday or as complex as a religious observance. Ask, "How are our lives richer because we have friends from different cultures?"

• The Jewish traditions in the story may be new to some of your students. Make a list of the Jewish traditions that Mrs. Katz shares in this story with Larnel so that your students benefit from her culture too. (They include the Yiddish name of Tush; the kugel as a snack; gefilte fish at the Seder meal; matzoh; saying kaddish for a deceased person; placing a small rock on a headstone in remembrance; the words *Shalom*, *bubeleh*, *kattileh*, *chuppa*, *bubee*, and *Mazel tov*; the seven-candle candlestick holder; the Seder meal; the celebration of Passover; the different sets of dishes used for Passover; and the lighting of two candles at the Seder supper.)

Transition Education Links

This story links well with objectives in Chapter 6, "Personal and Cultural Identity." Each main character in this story has his or her own cultural as well as personal identity. It was what makes them unique and special. Ask your students how this story would have changed if both of the main characters had been Jewish or African American. Why is the story stronger because they are not from the same cultural background? Ask your students if they could become one of the characters in the story, which elements would change to reflect their own cultural identity?

LESSON PLAN, GRADES 3–5

Amber Brown is Not a Crayon
by Paula Danziger

Synopsis

Amber Brown and Justin Daniels are two third graders who have been best friends since preschool. They help each other, stick up for each other and have great fun together. When Justin learns he is moving to Alabama, their relationship begins to change. Amber and Justin quarrel, and end up not speaking to each other until they finally find a way to work it out.

Objectives

1. To provide students with the opportunity to explore the ways friends can be both alike and different
2. To provide students with the opportunity to learn more about friendship and what it means to be a friend
3. To provide students with the opportunity to develop ways to make and keep friends
4. To provide students with the opportunity to identify ways to continue friendships after someone has moved away
5. To provide students with the opportunity to develop empathy for those who are moving away, staying behind, or arriving in a new community, and to explore ways to reach out and support them

Activities Before Reading

• Ask your students to think about a time when they were separated from a special friend because they moved or the friend moved away. Invite the children to share their feelings. Consider sharing your own experiences if they are relevant. Explain that in this story Amber and Justin grapple with the feelings involved when a best friend moves away. Acknowledge that when a friend moves, both the person who is leaving and the one staying behind are affected by the move. Ask your students if they think it is easier to leave or be the one left behind.

Activities After Reading

• Have students lead a literature discussion in small groups and talk about the ways Amber and Justin are alike and different. Ask each group to complete a Venn diagram. Ask them to think about a good friend of theirs and the ways they are alike and different. Do the differences complement or detract from the friendship, or make no difference at all?

Continue in small groups. Ask the students how they can tell Amber and Justin are good friends. (They know what each other is thinking, like each other just as they are, have fun together, and help each other out.) What are the qualities they look for and appreciate in their friends? Do these qualities guide them in choosing new friends when they move to a new place?

• Discuss the meaning of *empathy* with your class and ask for examples of empathy from the children's experiences. Ask, "How can you tell that Brandi has empathy for Amber and understands how she feels about Justin's leaving?" (She tells Jimmy to leave Amber alone when he teases her about Justin while he is away on a house-hunting trip. She also gives Hannah a shove and looks over at Amber when Hannah asks Justin if there are other kids near his new house because she knows Amber feels bad about his leaving.) Have your students write about a time they showed empathy for someone and about a time someone showed empathy for them. Ask them to include how they felt in each situation, being on both the giving and receiving ends. Respond to each child's piece.

• Brainstorm things they could do to make someone feel better if the person were missing a friend who moved away. (They might acknowledge the person's feelings or include them in a game or other activity.)

• When Justin arrives in Alabama he will be the new kid and will probably be nervous about making new friends and finding his way around. What are some ways other kids could welcome him to their new school and neighborhood?

• Why was Amber so angry about the chewing-gum ball? (It is something she and Justin had made together and represented their friendship.) Why do you think Amber thought the gum ball was the best present ever? Is there something you and a friend have made together that might be a special reminder of your friendship if he or she moved away? Brainstorm ideas for meaningful gifts your students might give to a friend who is leaving.

• In Chapter 8, Amber's mother talks to her about what is going on between Amber and Justin. Her mother says, "Sometimes when people have to leave each other, they act as if it isn't happening or they pick a fight so it won't seem so hard to go. In this case, it looks like both. But think of all the good times you and Justin are missing right now because you've stopped talking" (pp. 67–68). Discuss this with your students. What do they think of this and why? Explain that this is a common reaction for many people.

• Let your students know that although it can be difficult to share their feelings with others, it is important to be able to talk to their friends honestly in order to have a real friendship. Good communication is a key ingredient in any relationship. At the end of the story, Justin and Amber finally talk outside of their classroom. Have your students read the Readers' Theatre script of that encounter included below. Then ask them to write their own script when Amber and Justin say their final good-bye. They can set the scene at the airport, Amber's house, in the Daniels' driveway, or wherever they choose. Have each student perform their script with a partner.

Readers' Theatre for Amber Brown is Not a Crayon

Amber and Justin: I'm sorry.
Amber: I don't want you to go.
Justin: I don't want to go either. You think this is easy? My new school is so big. I don't know anyone there. What if I forget my locker combination? All the kids there already know each other. My parents say I have to be brave, be a good example for Danny. That it will be fun. But I know my mom is nervous about moving, too. I heard her talking to your mom. And it's too late to join the Little League team, and everyone there thinks I talk funny and I have to learn to say y'all and ma'am and . . . and . . .
Amber: And?
Justin: And I'm going to miss you.
Amber: Why didn't you tell me sooner?
Justin: Because you stopped talking to me.
Amber: You wouldn't talk to me. Not about the important stuff.
Justin: It's hard.
Amber: I want you to stay.
Justin: Me, too. But I can't. My parents are making me go. But they said you and your mom could visit this summer.
   (Justin gives Amber the gum ball present.)
Amber: Thanks. It's the best present ever. (pp. 75–77)

Suggested Follow-up Activities

• Have your class design a "Friendship" bulletin board. Your students can create posters advertising ways to be a good friend, including suggestions for reaching out to children who are new or missing old friends. Encourage them to include artwork and original poetry about friendship as well. Show your students examples of photographs that capture friendship. Purchase single-use cameras and have your students work as photojournalists to document friendship in your school. Include a display of their photographs as well.

• Have the students write an advice column on moving for your school or class newspaper, including ways to keep in touch with their classmates.

Transition Education Links

This story links with objectives in Chapter 2, "The Common Experience of Mobility." When Justin finally talks to Amber he expresses his worries and concerns about moving to Alabama: He doesn't know anyone; he might forget his locker combination; the new school is big; and it's too late to join Little League. Ask your students to brainstorm ways Justin could address these worries. (He might get a floor plan of the school, practice on a combination lock, explore other after-school activities that are offered, and make an effort to meet other kids on his block.) Provide an opportunity for your students to voice the worries and concerns they had when they moved and the ways they addressed them.

It also has links with Chapter 3, "The Process of Transition." After Justin returned from the house-hunting trip to Alabama, he realized he would have to adapt to different things once he moved. His new school is big, people speak differently, and he wouldn't be able to take part in Little League. Explain that there is usually a period of adjustment when moving to a new place. Help your students explore useful strategies to ease the move to a new location. (See Appendix E.)

Amber has experienced a great deal of loss in her life. Her parents are divorced, her father is working in France for a year, and now Justin is leaving. Be sensitive to the fact that some of your students may come from divorced families; in fact, a divorce may be the reason for their move. Discuss ways Amber might cope with her feelings. Perhaps she can talk with her mother, or draw or write in a journal. Help your students discover things they can do to manage their feelings of sadness and loss.

There are also links with Chapter 4, "Personal and Cultural Identity." Amber and Justin's teacher, Mr. Cohen, has the class "travel" to the different countries they study. They even create their own passports. Have your students choose their home country or another country they have lived in to research and report on to the class. The children can create travel posters or brochures, and you can have your students travel around the world stopping off at the different destinations. Food and clothing, music, and other aspects of culture can be incorporated into each child's presentation. This project provides an opportunity for your students to share their cultural backgrounds or knowledge of other places they have lived.

You can also have your students create a "cultural passport." Ask them to design a stamp from each country or place they have lived and draw a picture showing some part of the culture that influenced their lives. Children who have not moved can include places they have visited as well as where they live.

This story links well with Chapter 6, "Problem-Solving Skills." Discuss the way Amber and Justin resolved their conflict. (Amber used humor to break the ice with Justin, and he then took the risk to finally share his feelings.) Have your students write a journal entry about a time they had a conflict with a friend and how it got resolved. Respond to their solution.

LESSON PLAN, GRADES 3–5

The Kid in the Red Jacket
by Barbara Park

Synopsis

Howard Jeeter cannot believe it: He is going to be the new kid! Howard and his family are moving across the country from Arizona to Massachusetts, and he is convinced they are ruining his life. Desperate for a friend and missing his old friends, he is befriended by a 6-year-old girl who lives across the street. As a fifth grader, Howard is embarrassed to be seen with Molly and worries endlessly about what the other kids will think. As the story unfolds, Howard learns about empathy and friendship, and the process of adjusting to life in a new place. Told with humor and insight, this is a funny and poignant account of a child's experience of moving.

Objectives

1. To provide students with the opportunity to learn about the ways people are alike and different
2. To provide students with the opportunity to develop effective skills to establish and maintain friendships
3. To provide students with the opportunity to explore the nature of friendships and relationships
4. To provide students with the opportunity to explore ways to keep in touch after someone has moved away

5. To provide students with the opportunity to develop empathy for those who are moving away, staying behind, or arriving in a new community

Activities Before Reading

• Ask your students what it was like when they were a new kid at school and in the neighborhood. How did they feel and why? If you are willing, share your feelings and experiences when you were a new teacher at your school. Together with your students, compile a list of the feelings expressed.

• Explain that this story is about a fifth grader, Howard Jeeter, who moves from Arizona to Massachusetts in the United States. Ask your students why they think the author chose the title *The Kid in the Red Jacket* for this book. How might this describe the experience of being new?

Activities After Reading

• Ask your students to list the feelings Howard had when he moved. (He was furious at his parents and his father's company, sad at leaving his friends, scared, lonely when he had no one to eat lunch with or play with at recess, and embarrassed when he didn't know where to get milk or throw his trash away in the cafeteria.) Compare these to the feelings of your students charted earlier, and add them to the list.

• Give each of your students an outline of a red jacket and ask them to design it to show the things they would like others to know about them when they move. For example, they could include their name, an instrument they play, sports or activities they enjoy, or brothers or sisters they have. Have them transform the red jacket into a representation of their individual selves. Encourage them to be as creative as possible using words, phrases, drawings, painting, cutouts, and so on. Nonmobile students can design their jackets to show the things they would like new students to know about them.

• We often wait for others to reach out to us when we move, but it is important to know that we can reach out to others too. What are some things Howard could have done to make new friends? (He could have invited a classmate over to his house, started a conversation at lunch, or inquired about a soccer team at school since he played on a team in Arizona.)

• One of the hardest things Howard had to do was say good-bye to his best friends, Roger and Thornberry. Discuss the following questions: What were the hardest things you had to do when you moved? How can Howard keep in touch with his friends back in Arizona? How do you keep in touch with your friends who live in other places?

• Have your students write a letter to a friend back home describing what their new place is like. As in Howard's letter to Thornberry, include the differences between the two places. Howard was honest about how he was doing. Point out that it takes time to settle into a new place and it is OK to let your friends and family know that you are still getting used to it.

• Discuss the word *empathy*. What does it mean? Howard developed empathy for what it is like to be the new kid. He also developed empathy for Molly's losses and need for friendship. What examples from the book show he has empathy? Ask your students for examples of what empathy looks like. In what ways have you developed empathy as a result of moving or other life experiences? How have you acted on your empathy? In what ways can you show empathy to children who have newly arrived in your school or neighborhood and help them fit in?

• At the beginning of the book, Howard doesn't even want to see pictures of his new house. Explain that some people think that if they show an interest in or like the new place, they are not being loyal to the people and the place they are leaving. This can be very confusing for some people. Do you think you can like more than one place?

• Have your students work in pairs to chart the ways that Howard and Molly are alike and different. Make sure they include that they both suffered losses—for Howard, his old life in Arizona, and for Molly, her parents through their divorce. Which are most important, the differences or similarities between people? Why?

• Howard eventually grows fond of Molly. Discuss the following questions with your students: What do you think he learned about friendships and relationships? Is there a message in the friendship that Howard develops with Molly? What are the different types of friendships and relationships you can have? What makes someone a friend?

• Howard wants to be accepted by the other boys in his class. He therefore goes along with Ollie's game and hurts Molly's feelings by playing "keep away" with her favorite doll. Pete, on the other hand, speaks out against what they had done. Howard feels bad that he had gone along with the game even though he knew it wasn't the right thing to do. In a philosophy or sharing circle, have your students discuss what it means to be an "independent thinker." What are the risks of speaking your mind and saying what is true for you? Are they risks worth taking? Do you ever try to be like someone else? Why? How have you felt when you have followed your heart? When you have gone along with the crowd?

• Howard realizes that while Ollie is funny, they do not have much in common. He pauses to think about the qualities he is looking for in a friend. Acknowledge that making new friends is a worry and concern for all people who move, but it is important to think about the kinds of people we choose for friends. Have your students work in pairs to design a poster or brochure, or film a video about ways to choose new friends.

Suggested Follow-up Activities

• Help your students see that moving to a new place need not mean they lose friends, but can actually widen their circle of friends. The friendships that are important can be sustained over time and distance, but they require time and effort.

• Knowing what he knows now, how would Howard act toward the new kid at his old school? Have your students write a conversation between the two of them. They might include some conversation with Roger and Thornberry as well.

• Howard is angry at his parents about the move, and he complains and makes life difficult. Point out that the move is probably difficult for his parents as well. Even though he is angry, are there things he can do to help his family through this transition while at the same time acknowledging his real feelings? How have you been helpful when your family has had to move?

Transition Education Links

This story has links with objectives in Chapter 2, "The Common Experience of Mobility." Howard worries about what the kids would be like, whether he would fit in, and whether they would dress the same. Provide an opportunity for your students to share the worries or concerns they had when they moved.

This story also has links with objectives in Chapter 3, "The Process of Transition." It provides a good opportunity to teach children about the different stages in the transition process. Use the ADAPT model described in Chapter 3 to relate Howard's experiences to the different stages. As the story begins, Howard has just moved from the "Don't want to go, or do I?" stage (Leaving Stage) and is in the "Anything is possible!" stage (Transition Stage) en route to Massachusetts. As time passes and he begins to make new friends, he moves into the "Perhaps this isn't so bad" stage (Entering Stage). Have your students find passages from the book that illustrate his feelings in each of these stages.

Howard experienced many different feelings, but it was a deep sense of sadness that was most powerful. What might have made Howard feel better? (Perhaps he could have phoned his friends.) What are some things you can do when you are sad? Suggestions might include allowing yourself to cry, talking with your parents, keeping a journal, and realizing that you just have to give the new situation time.

Howard experiences culture shock moving within his own country, as the lifestyle in Arizona is very different than in Massachusetts. What are some of the things Howard must adjust to? (The houses look different, the weather is colder, he has to wear winter clothing, the names of streets are different, and his school looks different.) Teach your students about the experience of culture shock. Discuss the things they had to get used to when they moved to their present location.

Howard's father says, "You'll make friends, son. You'll make them. Meanwhile, why don't you just give this place a chance, okay?" (p. 22). What additional advice would you give to Howard on ways to approach the changes he is facing?

This story has links to Chapter 6, "Problem-Solving Skills." Discuss ways to resolve conflict and mend relationships with others.

> Have your students complete the following sentence starters:
> When I do something that hurts someone, I feel_____.
> When I apologize, I feel_____.
> When I do not apologize and admit I made a mistake, I feel _____.
> When someone apologizes to me, I feel _____.

Acknowledge that admitting we are wrong and saying "I'm sorry" is one of the hardest things to do, yet it is one of the most important in order to resolve a conflict. Howard eventually apologizes to Molly for throwing her doll. He recognized that saying "I'm sorry" was not enough, and he tried to explain his actions. Discuss ways to say "I'm sorry" and resolve a conflict with someone. Ask your students to write about a time when they apologized to someone and when someone apologized to them.

LESSON PLAN, GRADE 5

Beyond the Mango Tree
by Amy Bronwen Zemser

Synopsis

Sarina is an American girl whose family has moved from Boston, Massachusetts, to the country of Liberia in Africa. Sarina's mother, who is sick, has not adjusted at all to the move and is constantly afraid for Sarina's safety. Occasionally she will tie Sarina to the mango tree in their yard so that Sarina will not stray off the property. Eventually Sarina meets Boima, a local boy who becomes her trusted friend. Together they often explore the world outside the mango tree, and Sarina comes to understand the meaning of true friendship. (Note: The author lived in Liberia for 3 years as a child.)

Objectives

1. To provide students with the opportunity to learn about the ways people are alike and different
2. To provide students with the opportunity to develop effective skills to establish and maintain friendships
3. To provide students with the opportunity to explore the cultural differences that can exist within friendships, and that can also enrich them.
4. To provide students with the opportunity to explore ways to reach out to welcome newcomers in the community

Activities Before Reading

• Ask your students to think of a good friend they have had in their life. Ask students to think of all the characteristics that made this person their friend. Ask them to write down on slips of paper the different characteristics or qualities that this friend had, or memories they shared. Then give lunch bags to the children to put the slips of paper in. You can help them get started by modeling your own thoughts. For example, you might think aloud: "Well, Alison was my best friend when I lived in New Jersey. We would walk home from school together each day and tell each other all our secrets. I remember we would always stop in the bakery and buy a glazed doughnut to eat on the way home. On my first slip of paper I could write, 'I could trust her with my secrets.' Then on another slip of paper I could write, 'We liked the same things,' and I could also write, 'We liked being together.'"

• Have them keep the bag in their desks while you read this novel aloud. Ask them to think about their own special friend as they listen to the story of Sarina and the special friendship that developed in her life. Tell them that at the conclusion of the novel everyone will share their lunch bags in a special way.

During the reading

• This story has many emotive parts that most likely will trigger student discussion. Invite your students to comment about the action or plot at any point in the story. Help them to refrain from judging the characters' actions and to discuss instead how Sarina's friendship with Boima grew as a result of her need for a friend.

Activities After Reading

- From the very beginning of the story there are many cultural differences between Sarina and Boima. Have your students chart the differences with you. (They spoke different languages; Boima is African, while Sarina is American; and he works in the marketplace, while she stays at the house with her mother.) Then have everyone look at the chart and decide which differences really do not matter and which differences can be potential obstacles in a friendship. (A language barrier can be a potential obstacle, while different nationalities may not be obstacles.) Continue a discussion with your students about potential obstacles to friendships and how people can overcome them.
- Then make a second chart of the similarities between Sarina and Boima. (They both wanted a friend; they were both about the same age; they both liked to explore.) Continue from the first discussion and talk about why similarities are important to friendships. (They give the friends common ground in the relationship.)
- Ask your students how the friendship began and what the children actually did to establish the beginning of a relationship. (They talked to each other, asked each other their names, and offered a gesture of kindness by helping each other.) Then ask the students how those skills can relate to their own lives. In order to find a friend what are some of the things you need to do? (Suggestions might include you need to reach out, be communicative, be friendly, be helpful, and so on.)
- Sometimes people who have moved a lot are reluctant to make friends because it hurts when that friend moves on without them. In this story, the end of the friendship is much sadder because Boima became fatally ill and there wasn't anything that Sarina could do to save his life. While this part in the story is very sad, it is important to talk with the students about the value of forming friendships, regardless of what the future may hold. It is friendships and relationships that nurture and sustain us in life, and for children who move frequently, new friendships can ease the transition process. Ask your students to suppose what Sarina's life in Liberia would have been like if she had never met Boima.
- Sarina also had a relationship with the adult servants in her home: Te Te and Thomas Scott. What are the advantages of having adult acquaintances? What are the disadvantages of not having friends your same age? How did Te Te act as a friend to help Sarina? Would Sarina have been able

to become friends with Boima if Te Te had not helped her? Te Te, however, is also a friend to Boima, and Sarina does not understand their relationship. Ask your students why Sarina is so angry that Te Te helped steal food for Boima. Is it that sometimes when we finally find a friend, we don't want to share him or her with others? Continue this discussion and help your students see that it is possible to have multiple relationships. Encourage them to be understanding when one of their friends has a special relationship with someone else as well as with them.

• Why do your students suppose that Sarina really didn't understand Boima's lifestyle and how poor his family was? When she finds out about how Te Te stole the boney fish for Boima, she only gets angry at Boima without really thinking about the motive behind the theft. Does this mean that even with best friends we don't always understand how they live and what their life is like? How can your students practice being less judgmental of their peers and of other cultures? Talk about the qualities of empathy and acceptance, when not everyone else's family has the same lifestyle as yours.

• Ask your students why Sarina's mother did not want her playing with the native children or going to a local school. Your students will probably respond that Sarina's mother was prejudiced. Ask them to speculate why it is that people sometimes fear other people who are different from them. Help your students see that people are often most afraid of things that they do not understand. If Sarina's mother had taken the time to meet Boima and get to know him as a person, then perhaps she would have better understood the people of Liberia and not had a fear or distrust of the native children. Talk about the stereotypes we sometimes hold in our minds about people from other cultures to extend this idea further.

• Another important concept in this story is how Boima helped Sarina learn to appreciate living in Africa. In the beginning of the story she is lonely and somewhat timid because of the constant rain and her mother's fears. Her first attempt in learning more about the community is when she asks Te Te to take her to the Joe Bar market. The real reason she begins to explore her community is because Boima meets her and shows her things about the community she might not otherwise learn. Ask your students how they could reach out to a new student in their community, and what they could do to help that student learn about the community.

Suggested Follow-up Activities

• Once you have finished the story, host a lunch for your students as a culminating activity to the novel. Have the students bring the lunch bag containing the character traits and memories of their friend, as well as a real lunch. Tell your students to first open their bags of friendship strips and arrange them on their desks. Then ask if anyone listed a trait that was similar to a trait that either Sarina or Boima possessed. Give students time to share from their bags, and then have lunch together. Encourage students to bring in one food from their own ethnic background, or a food that is indigenous to the community where they are currently living—just like mangoes were indigenous to Liberia.

Transition Education Links

This story also links to Chapter 3, "The Process of Transition." Sarina had to adapt to many changes when she moved from Massachusetts to Liberia, such as the geography, the climate, and the culture. While Sarina was open to learning about the culture, she began to adjust to her new life more readily once she and Boima became friends. Ask your students to describe how they made a new friend to help them adjust to a new country and culture. Are there other strategies they used that made the adjustment easier?

Sarina's mother experienced extreme culture shock, which affected Sarina's adjustment to life in Liberia. Help your students learn more about the experience of culture shock. Explain that people respond differently to the experience of moving, and sometimes children are affected by their parents' stress. However, family members can help each other to adjust. Discuss ways Sarina's family could have helped each other. Perhaps they could have talked with each other about how they were feeling about their new life in Liberia. Highlight the importance of communication among family members and the importance of validating your feelings about a move by sharing both your concerns and the delights you have found in the new culture. Have your students share the things they do or can do to ease the transition for their entire family. This may include offering to help or being particularly responsible when asked to do things.

This story also has links with Chapter 6, "Problem-Solving Skills." Sarina finds out that Te Te helped Boima steal food from her family. Although she was his friend, she hardly noticed that he was hungry, and she didn't understand that his pride kept him from asking for help. Her anger kept her from really seeing him, and then it was too late to resolve the conflict once he became ill. What could Sarina have done to solve the problem between them?

Invite your students to share a situation where they had a misunderstanding with a friend. How did they resolve it? Ask your students what they think Sarina learned from this experience.

IDEAS FOR CROSS-CURRICULAR CONNECTIONS

Creative and Performing Arts

Have your students create a multimedia "Friendship" collage. Have them bring photographs of their friends, draw pictures, or make cutouts. When they are ready to assemble their collage, give each student a large piece of art paper and have them draw a fist-sized symbol of friendship in the center of the paper. For example, they may choose to draw the outline of a heart. Then in the middle of the symbol ask them to write a few words that define the meaning of friendship to them. They may choose words like *trust*, *understanding*, *helpful*, and so on. Brainstorm possible word choices and let them choose the ones that appeal to them. Display the collages around the classroom.

Encourage your students to write songs about friendship. They could also mime different activities they would do with a friend.

Social Studies

Have your students create journals or letters that someone in history might have penned to a friend that was left behind or who stayed at home. For example, a soldier during a particular war might have written letters to a friend back home, or a pioneer might have kept a journal of his or her travels as they ventured forth to a new home. Imaginary letters can be written by immigrants who leave friends behind, describing the new country to the friends who still live back home.

Science

As part of a study of plants, explore the conditions that help relationships thrive as well. Ask your students what plants need in order to grow (sunlight, water, food, soil). Conduct a class experiment and grow seedlings under varying conditions with only one seedling given the optimum growing conditions. Have the class observe the seedlings over the course of 10 days to see what happens. Discuss how relationships are like plants. Establish that friendships need to be tended and nurtured just like plants, or they can wither from lack of attention.

People and places have a lasting effect on our lives, and in the same way we can have a lasting effect in our community. Discuss the idea of making a difference in whatever community you live in for however long you might be there. Encourage your students to think of ways they can show care and concern to the school or local community by making a difference to the environment. Perhaps they could begin or maintain a recycling program that will continue long after they move again. They might plant bulbs to beautify the school, create a school garden, or take care of local wildlife. Help your students see the value in what we can all contribute.

Math

Ask your students to survey their classmates to discover what they have in common and present their findings to the class. They may choose to collect data on places they have lived, number of languages spoken, favorite pets, hobbies, colors, or books. They can use the computer to generate different ways to represent their data.

Chapter 6

Problem-Solving Skills

Developing competency in managing change, solving problems, making decisions, resolving conflicts, managing stress, and communicating with others are essential life skills for everyone. In our daily lives we encounter situations that require making choices and decisions, getting along with others, and finding solutions to various problems. Children who move are adjusting to a wide range of new circumstances, and well-developed life skills are a tremendous asset.

It is important to create authentic opportunities for your students to learn and practice these skills daily. Not only is it important to help your students continue to develop effective life skills, it is important for them to see how they can be used in helping themselves and others. This enables children to develop a sense of their own competence. Many children develop and use effective life skills, yet they are often unaware that they have them.

Help children build on the successes they have already experienced. Provide opportunities for them to discuss some of the changes in their lives, and help them identify times when they have managed change well or made positive decisions. Build on the skills your students are learning through their mobile lifestyles. For example, children with multicultural perspectives are usually excellent mediators, as they are able to see an issue from different sides. Help your students identify and develop their individual strengths.

Children need opportunities to learn and practice decision-making skills. Making life decisions helps them develop a sense of identity and confidence. Children also need to be able to share their feelings with others, state their needs clearly, and listen to others. With these skills they can learn to work their way through problems and arrive at reasonable and fair solutions, resolving conflicts that may arise.

It is important for all children to develop effective skills to approach cross-cultural adaptation and to communicate across cultures. Help your students learn to observe differences and behaviors without judging them or generalizing about groups of people. Foster an openness toward learning how and why people do what they do.

Effective leave-taking skills are also among the most important skills we can learn. Moving away and leaving people and places that were meaningful is particularly difficult. It is paramount for children and their families to take time to plan their good-byes and draw closure in a place before they move. Regret over lost opportunities can stay with adults and children for a long time. David Pollock (1999) has developed the RAFT strategy which is a useful approach to leaving (see Figure 6.1). It is helpful to actually devise a moving plan with your students to ensure that closure takes place.

FIGURE 6.1. RAFT Strategy

Reconciliation
Affirmation
Farewells
Think ahead

The **R** is for Reconciliation, or Resolving any conflicts that may exist with someone.

The **A** is for Affirmation, or expressing thanks to friends, family, neighbors, and others who have shared in our lives.

The **F** is for Farewells, and we are encouraged to say farewell to important people, places, and even things we have enjoyed. For children, this could be a favorite rope swing or hiding place.

The **T** is for Think Ahead. People are encouraged to begin to plan ahead for their new location.

In explaining this concept to young children, the **R** can be explained as Making Things Right, and the **A** as showing Appreciation.

R Making things Right
A Appreciation
F Farewells
T Think ahead

CONCEPTS FEATURED IN ACTIVITIES

1. *Effective interpersonal and life skills can ease the experience of transition.* Developing effective interpersonal and life skills can give children confidence in their ability to manage change and adapt to new situations. When children see themselves as competent and able to make sound decisions, resolve conflicts, solve problems, and develop relationships with other people, they begin to know that they can handle new situations that arise. Acquiring life skills and strategies to approach change helps them develop the inner resources they can draw on during times of transition throughout their lives. Children learn to take care of themselves physically, mentally, and emotionally, and are also able to develop healthy and satisfying relationships with others.

2. *Effective cross-cultural skills are necessary in our diverse society.* People from numerous cultures live and work together in communities around the world. This rich diversity can offer each of us so much; yet all too often cultural difference is met with fear and apprehension rather than the understanding that would engender respect and appreciation. For people to live and work together peaceably and productively, we all need to develop cross-cultural awareness, understanding, sensitivity, and communication skills. These are essential skills so that we can break down barriers between people, counter racism, and celebrate our common humanity. Children are naturally receptive to new learning, and it is essential to help them begin to develop these skills as early as possible.

3. *Appropriate closure is necessary for successful adjustment to a new location.* Research has confirmed the importance of drawing closure in the place we are leaving before we can successfully adjust to the one we are going to. In his book *The Way of Transition* (2001), William Bridges has written about the need for endings before there can be new beginnings. Children can learn effective ways to leave the people and places that have been a part of their lives, and you can support and encourage their efforts. Provide opportunities for your students to think of meaningful ways they could say good-bye. It is important to be aware that parents may think it is best for their child to move on as quickly as possible, usually because that is the parents' way of handling the situation. You can provide opportunities for your class to say good-bye to a student who is leaving by providing transition activities such as making a memory book, or having the class sign a T-shirt. This honors the time that you all shared together in a special way.

Due to individual family circumstances, some children may not have the opportunity to say good-bye to you or their classmates. If this is the case, you can help them draw closure after they have left by having your students send notes, cards, poems, or photographs. It is important to emphasize that closure is as important for the children staying behind as for the ones that are leaving.

Objectives: To provide students with the opportunity

- to discuss and develop strategies for managing change
- to learn steps for effective decision making and problem solving
- to learn ways to resolve conflicts and mend relationships
- to practice effective communication skills including cross-cultural communication
- to explore ways to say good-bye effectively

LESSON PLAN, GRADES 3–5

Chicken Sunday
by Patricia Polacco

Synopsis

Patricia and her two best friends, Winston and Stewart, want to surprise the boys' grandmother, Miss Eula Mae, by buying her a special church hat for Easter. They know the hat she wants is in Mr. Kodinski's hat shop, but none of them have enough money to buy it. When they decide to go to Mr. Kodinski's shop and ask for a part-time job, they are wrongfully accused of vandalism. They can't tell Miss Eula Mae the truth or they will ruin the surprise of trying to buy the hat, so they must solve the problem together to come up with a solution.

Objectives

1. To provide students with the opportunity to learn effective problem-solving skills
2. To provide students with the opportunity to learn about effective communication skills, including cross-cultural communication
3. To provide students with the opportunity to learn ways to resolve conflicts

Activities Before Reading

- If this is the first book written by Patricia Polacco that you are sharing with your class, take time to introduce the author and teach your students about her unique past. This will not only help them better understand *Chicken Sunday*, but will also give them an appreciation of how Ms. Polacco's childhood experiences influenced her career as an illustrator and an author.

Background on Patricia Polacco: Born into a bicultural family, her mother's family was Ukrainian and her father's family was Italian. Patricia was born in Michigan and then moved as a young child to Oakland, California. It was in Oakland that she became best friends with Stewart and Winston Washington, the two African American characters in *Chicken Sunday*. School was not easy for Patricia, and her cultural background was very different from most of her classmates, but she was always excellent in art. Her Ukrainian grandmother taught her the ancient art of making pysanky eggs, where the artist makes detailed designs in hot wax on the egg before dyeing it different colors. When Ms. Polacco grew up and decided to write children's books, she retold stories from her own childhood and often used her family and childhood friends as models for the characters. Almost every picture book she has designed and written has been autobiographical.

• Ask your students to listen closely and study the illustrations as you read *Chicken Sunday*. Ask them to see if they can find any details in the book that might have actually come from Ms. Polacco's childhood.

Activities After Reading

• Use the following list to discuss the details in the book that really did come from Ms. Polacco's life.

1. Stewart and Winston Washington really were her best friends.
2. Miss Eula Mae Washington was the boys' grandmother.
3. Patricia did go to Miss Eula Mae's house for Sunday dinners.
4. Patricia taught Winston and Stewart how to make pysanky eggs.
5. The children did get wrongly accused of vandalizing the hat shop.
6. The children did go to talk to Mr. Kodinski, and then were allowed to sell their decorated eggs in his shop.
7. Mr. Kodinski did give them the Easter hat for Miss Eula Mae.
8. The photographs on the page with Miss Eula Mae and the children having Sunday dinner are the real photographs of Miss Eula Mae's family.
9. The illustration of Mr. Kodinski having tea with the children shows a number tattooed on his arm, indicating that he was a Holocaust survivor.

• Now discuss how Patricia, Winston, and Stewart went about try-ing to solve their dilemma about buying Miss Eula Mae the hat. What were the steps that led to their successful resolution?

1. They worked cooperatively as a group.
2. First they assessed the situation. (They counted the money they had al-ready saved.)
3. Then they brainstormed ideas. (They decided to ask Mr. Kodinski for jobs.)
4. When their first idea did not work out, they began brainstorming again.
5. They used clear communication to state their needs.
6. They looked at their problem from different perspectives. (They saw the situation from Mr. Kodinski's perspective.)
7. They chose an alternative idea—making the eggs—which turned out to be a successful resolution.

• Ask your students why the children were successful with Mr. Kodinski. What communication skills did they use that helped them both resolve the conflict and also solve the problem? (They looked at the situation from Mr. Kodinski's perspective; they told him the truth; they listened to his side of the story; they were open-minded about new ideas; and they tried to reach a compromise both sides could agree on.) You and your students could draft a list of similar steps for effective communi-cation that could be used in your classroom whenever a conflict arises that needs to be resolved. Point out that the children stood up for them-selves and told the truth, but also took action to make things right with Mr. Kodinski. It took courage to go to see him, but it was the right thing to do.

• The painted eggs were a "peace offering" to Mr. Kodinski. Discuss with your students that sometimes you can give a small gift as part of re-solving a conflict with someone. Explain that rather than a purchased gift, it could be something you made or a kind note or card. It could simply be the offer of a handshake of friendship.

• Discuss the ways the children in the story develop cross-cultural awareness and cross-cultural communication skills. In the beginning of the story, Winnie is fearful about approaching Mr. Kodinski for work as he says he is strange, never smiles, and looks mean. After spending an afternoon talking together, having tea and cake, and telling each other about their lives, the children and Mr. Kodinski get to know each other. What do you think the children and Mr. Kodinski learned about each other? In what ways might the children now have a better understanding of Mr. Kodinski and his life? Discuss the approaches they used. (They took time to listen and were open to learning about each other.) Discuss ways people can address their fears when they meet people who are different. (Suggestions might include being open to learning about their culture and themselves as individuals, and refraining from judgment.)

Suggested Follow-up Activities

• The title of this book is very appropriate because the special relationship that Ms. Polacco had with Miss Eula Mae centered on the experience of having Sunday suppers at Miss Eula Mae's home. The fact that Miss Eula Mae always served a special meal of chicken led Patricia Polacco to think of those occasions as "Chicken Sundays." Ask your students to think of a special meal that they have when visiting relatives or friends, or that someone in their own home prepares for festive occasions. Ask them to write a journal entry just describing that meal, the occasion, and the people involved. You may want to model this first with a memory from your own life. For example, a special springtime celebration entry might be entitled "Mint Jelly Chops" for a special yearly meal when mint jelly was served with spring lamb. Invite each child to read his or her piece to a peer or share it with the entire class.

• Apologizing for something is one of the hardest things for people of all ages to do. Have your students write role-play scenarios involving a conflict with someone where they hurt the other person's feelings or did something wrong. A true apology involves more than just saying "I'm sorry." Ask them to carefully think through the conversation they would have. Have each student read his or her scenario and choose other classmates to play the other parts. Have the students act them out for the rest of the class and discuss them.

Transition Education Links

This story links well with Chapter 4, "Personal and Cultural Identity." Miss Eula Mae, Stewart, and Winston are African American Baptists, and Mr. Kodinksi and Patricia Polacco are Russian Jews. Each character has unique cultural facets to their personality, background, and experiences that influence each other's lives. Provide opportunities for your students to discuss the cultural influences of people in their lives and the ways their culture has influenced others.

This story also links with Chapter 5, "Friendships and Relationships." Explore the ways cultural differences can enrich friendships. Ask your students to describe a relationship they have with a child from another culture. This person may be a friend, relative, classmate, or neighbor. Discuss the ways their lives are enriched by knowing them.

Patricia went to church with her friends. Ask your students if they have ever visited different houses of worship or participated in celebrations from other cultures or religions. What did they learn or find interesting?

LESSON PLAN, K–3

Chrysanthemum
by Kevin Henkes

Synopsis

Chrysanthemum is a little girl who absolutely loves her name until she starts school and the other children make fun of it. No matter how hard her parents try to help, the pressure of the other children is enormous, and soon Chrysanthemum doesn't want to go back to school. Eventually it is the music teacher, Mrs. Twinkle, who solves Chrysanthemum's dilemma.

Objectives

1. To provide students with the opportunity to discuss and develop strategies for managing change
2. To provide students with the opportunity to develop effective problem-solving skills
3. To provide students with the opportunity to develop ways to resolve conflict

Activities Before Reading

• Ask students to generate a list with you about the things that are worrisome about starting at a new school. This list might include making new friends, figuring out which bus to take, learning how to order food in the cafeteria, how to ask about going to the bathroom, and whether others will pronounce your name correctly. Then explain to the children that for almost every worry, there is a way to address it. For example, if you are unsure about which bus to take, perhaps your parents or an older sibling can go with you on the first day of school to make sure that you are at the right bus stop. By thinking through the problem and asking others for help, the problem may be resolved. Explain that pronouncing people's names correctly can be tricky. Children could practice saying their names slowly and clearly to help others learn them. You can then play a name game to reinforce this. Have the children sit in a circle. The first person to start says his or her name and then introduces the next person. Continue around the circle until everyone has been introduced.

• Names are very personal and often have special significance. In some cultures, names have particular meaning or are given in memory of other relatives. Invite your students to share how they were given their names. You might start the discussion by sharing how your name was decided for you. It is important that children learn to recognize that everybody's name should be honored. Explain that in this story a young girl finds herself faced with a dilemma because of her name.

Activities After Reading

• After reading the story, ask your class what Chrysanthemum might have done to help herself in her dilemma. Answers may range from ignoring Victoria, to changing her name, to adopting a nickname. The reality is, however, that there will always be children like Victoria who tease other children, particularly those who are vulnerable. In this story Chrysanthemum was teased because of her name. Children might also be teased because they wear glasses or come from another country, or dress differently. Let the children know it is an important life skill to learn how to solve problems and resolve conflicts. These are skills that both children and adults continue to learn throughout their lives. Perhaps Chrysanthemum could have been assertive and told Victoria that she did not like being teased, or she could have talked to her teacher about how she felt. Have your class suggest additional solutions. You might create an "If . . . Then . . . " poster. You post the "If" scenario, and your class provides the possible "Then" solutions. For example, If Victoria makes fun of Chrysanthemum in the lunch line, Then Chrysanthemum could . . . Use the examples from the book as well, such as If Victoria said, "If I had a name like yours, I'd change it," Then Chrysanthemum could say, "I like my name!"

• Discuss significant changes that have happened in your students' lives and how they managed them. When Chrysanthemum felt bad she talked to her parents, wore her favorite clothes that made her feel comfortable, and brought her good luck charms to school. Talk with your students about what they can do when they feel bad, are worried about something, or are adjusting to a new situation. Some ideas might include writing or drawing in a journal, exercising to feel better, talking to a parent, or even having a good cry. Explain that sometimes problems are not solved immediately, but take time to be resolved.

• This story provides a good opportunity to initiate a class discussion on peer pressure. Chrysanthemum allowed the behavior of some of her classmates to interfere with her enjoyment of going to school. At one point Chrysanthemum begins to dislike her name. Discuss how people in a new situation often want to change so that they fit in. Explain to your students that while it is understandable to adopt some cultural behaviors such as wearing popular clothing, it is important to retain their own cultural identity. Learning how to solve problems now will help your students solve more difficult problems later on.

• Talk with your students about having the courage to stand up for others when they see something wrong occurring. Point out that some of the other children in Chrysanthemum's class actually joined Victoria in teasing Chrysanthemum. What could the other children have done or said to Victoria when she was being so mean? Ask your students to describe a time when they saw someone stand up for another person or when they have done so themselves.

Suggested Follow-up Activities

• Have your students create special nameplates for their desk or table that highlight important things about them, such as their hobbies, favorite colors, and so on. This activity gives children a sense of pride in their name and allows them to express their own individuality. When guests visit your classroom, they can quickly see each child's name and also address them properly. It is very important that you yourself learn how to pronounce each child's name correctly.

• Discuss the reasons children tease each other. Ask, "How can we build each other up instead of bring each other down?" Have your students make a "Builder Upper" poster for your classroom that displays suggestions of encouraging and positive comments they can make to support each other.

Transition Education Links

This story links well with objectives in Chapter 5, "Friendships and Relationships." Help your students develop ways to establish friendships. Based on the book *Kids' Random Acts of Kindness* (1994), with a foreword by Rosalynn Carter, have your class create their own book describing situations they have observed where children or adults showed caring toward each other. You can add to the book throughout the year and share it with other classes in the school.

LESSON PLAN, GRADES K–5

Ira Says Goodbye
by Bernard Waber

Synopsis

Ira's best friend, Reggie, is moving away in just 2 weeks. Ira can't believe it! Reggie has been his best friend as far back as he can remember. Ira thinks of all the special things that he and Reggie have done together. Ira looks for Reggie and they talk about the move, but the next day Reggie is not the same Reggie. All he can think about and talk about is how great it will be to move to Greendale. Ira feels hurt and angry, and Reggie eventually expresses his sadness when both boys finally say good-bye. Both Ira and Reggie experience many of the feelings and reactions that arise when one friend moves away and the other is left behind.

Objectives

1. To provide students with the opportunity to discuss and develop strategies to manage change
2. To provide students with the opportunity to learn ways to resolve conflicts and mend relationships
3. To provide students with the opportunity to learn effective communication skills
4. To provide students with the opportunity to explore ways to say good-bye effectively

Activities Before Reading

• Introduce the topic of leave-taking, acknowledging both the feelings of those who leave and those who stay behind. Say, "When each of us moved here, we had to say good-bye to some very special people."

Have your students think of the people they had to say good-bye to and what they did to say good-bye. Have them share this with a partner. How did they feel? How did those staying behind feel? Have several students share their responses with the class.

• Introduce the story *Ira Says Goodbye*. Ask for predictions based on the title, cover, and your students' experiences.

Activities After Reading

• Discuss the story and explore the ways Ira and Reggie deal with the pain of Reggie's move. Include questions such as these: How did Ira feel when he first learned Reggie was moving? How did Reggie feel? How did Reggie's behavior change? Why do you think he reacted the way he did? What do you think of his reaction? Are there other ways he could have responded? How did this make Ira feel? How did Ira then react? Why? Have you ever felt like Ira or Reggie? What would you have done if you were Ira? Reggie? How did Ira and Reggie finally say good-bye to each other on moving day?

• Have your students work with a partner and brainstorm ways Ira and Reggie could have said good-bye well. Some ideas are as follows: They could have planned a last sleepover at Reggie's house, performed a farewell magic show with the Amazing Reggie and Fantastic Ira, talked with each other about how they really felt, made memory books, made a tape or video, put together photo albums, had photo T-shirts made, or planned ways to keep in touch.

• Explain to your students that people often create conflict with those who are leaving them or those they are leaving because they think it will be easier to leave or be left if they are angry with the person. However, unresolved conflicts cause even greater pain. Ira is hurt by Reggie's reaction and begins to find things he doesn't like about him. Discuss this. Let your students know that even though it may be difficult, it is important to learn how to express their feelings honestly. How might Ira share his true feelings with Reggie? Have students write a conversation between Ira and Reggie where they share their true feelings before Reggie leaves or as a continuation of the story when Ira visits him in Greendale. This could be performed as a role-play or Readers' Theatre.

• Both Ira and Reggie have many feelings as they deal with the changes in their lives due to Reggie's move. Discuss ways they could approach these changes. Some strategies might include writing or drawing in a journal, talking with their parents, or taking a risk and talking with each other about their feelings.

Suggested Follow-up Activities

- Have your students write or draw about a time they had to say good-bye to someone.
- Have partners choose a scene from the story to act out where Ira and Reggie share their real feelings with each other.
- Write and perform skits about saying good-bye, well and not so well.
- This is also an excellent opportunity to teach David Pollock's RAFT strategy as a way to say good-bye effectively. Have students work in small groups to chart suggestions for ways Reggie could have used the RAFT strategy. For example:

> *Reconciliation or Making Things Right*. Reggie and Ira could say they are sorry for hurting each other's feelings and share their true feelings with each other.
>
> *Affirmation or Appreciation*. Reggie could talk with his family, friends, neighbors, and teachers about the things he appreciates about them and the times they spent together. In particular, he could let Reggie know how much fun he had with him and what a good friend he has been.
>
> *Farewell*. Reggie could say good-bye to special places, (his house, garden, tree house, and secret hiding place with Ira), people (neighbors, teachers, and other children, and perhaps plan things he would like to do with Ira before he leaves), pets (his turtle), and possessions he might have to leave behind.
>
> *Think Ahead*. Reggie could think ahead and learn more about Greendale by asking questions and gathering information. He could find out about his new house, school, and neighborhood.

Have your students complete their own RAFT plan as if they were going to move. Is there anyone they would need to resolve a conflict with? What people and places have they appreciated, and who would they say thank-you to? Who and what would they say good-bye to? What would they want to know about their new destination?

Transition Education Links

This story has links with objectives in Chapter 3, "The Process of Transition." It provides children with the opportunity to explore the feelings that may arise and the reactions that may occur when one friend moves away and the other stays behind. Relate Ira and Reggie's feelings to those your students may have as well.

Let students know that it is particularly important to allow ourselves and others to express the grief we feel when we move or others move away. Unresolved grief has far-reaching effects and makes it more difficult to settle into the next location. Ira's family is sad when Reggie's family drives away. They go inside and bake a cake. While baking a cake may make them feel better, discuss other things they could do that might be more authentic given how they feel. For example, Ira's family might reminisce about the special times they had with Reggie's family, talk about how sad they feel, look at photographs they took together, or write a letter to them to send to their new house.

This story also explores some of the experiences people have as they go through the process of transition and the different transition stages. Once they know they are moving and enter the Leaving Stage, it is natural for people to disengage. People who are leaving usually begin to focus on the new location and those who are staying behind may pull away as well. However, there is a danger of pulling away too soon and missing time that could be spent together, and not gaining proper closure before leaving a place. Discuss this with your students and use this story as an opportunity to teach them about disengagement, both with those who are leaving and those who are staying behind. What feelings are associated with disengagement? Reggie disengages from Ira too soon and focuses only on moving to Greendale. What problems are caused by pulling away too soon? How does this make Ira feel? Has this ever happened to you? Have you ever pulled away too soon?

An effective strategy for managing transition is to learn about the new location before you arrive. People have the most difficulty moving to a new place when their expectations differ from the reality of their experience. Ask your students, "Are Reggie's expectations about moving to Greendale realistic? Why do you think he is only focusing on the positive? What expectations would be more realistic for him?" You can have your students chart their own expectations when they moved here to see which ones were the same as or different from their actual experience. What helped them have realistic expectations? Is there anything that would have helped their expectations be more realistic? What would they want to know when they move again?

This story also has links with objectives in Chapter 5, "Friendships and Relationships." It is unlikely that your students will be able to see their old friends as soon as in Ira's case. Discuss ways to keep in touch with friends when one is living far away. Have your students write and publish a guide or class book on "How to Keep in Touch with Friends." Be sensitive to children who may not be able to keep in touch with their friends due to circumstances in the country they left behind.

LESSON PLAN, K–5

Molly's Pilgrim
by Barbara Cohen

Synopsis

Molly is a young girl who has moved with her family from Russia to the United States. She has been teased by some of her fellow classmates because she appears different from them. When the teacher gives a Thanksgiving assignment to make a Pilgrim doll, Molly's mother makes a Russian doll to commemorate her own journey as a contemporary pilgrim. When Molly takes the doll to school, the other children laugh at it until Molly helps her teacher and her classmates understand that there are modern pilgrims as well as the Pilgrims who came to Plymouth Rock.

Objectives

1. To provide opportunities for students to learn steps for effective decision making and problem solving
2. To provide opportunities for students to learn ways to resolve conflict
3. To provide opportunities for students to learn effective communication skills, including cross-cultural communication

Activities Before Reading

   • Ask your students if they know what the word *Pilgrim* means. Start a "Then and Now" chart on the board, and have your students list ideas for the "Then" side of the chart by describing who the Pilgrims were and why they came to America in the 1600s. Explain to them that the word *pilgrim* refers to any person who undertakes a long journey to a distant place, often for religious reasons. Have them listen to the story so they will be able to complete the "Now" side of the chart.

Activities After Reading

   The most telling line in the book is the last sentence: "It takes all kinds of Pilgrims to make a Thanksgiving." Using that line help your students complete the "Now" side of the chart. Help them understand that even today people leave their homeland in search of religious freedom. Ask them to consider other reasons that someone would become a pilgrim and journey a great distance to find other kinds of freedoms. (Answers might include political freedom, economic opportunity, or a better way of life.)

• You may want to couple this story with Eve Bunting's *How Many Days to America,* which is a contemporary Thanksgiving story, also about modern pilgrims. Help your students see that there are many ethnic groups who pursue freedoms, not just the Pilgrims from Europe.

• Molly's mother was also a pilgrim adjusting to life in a new country. Ask your students to interview older members of their own family to find out what problems they had to solve when they first came to a new country. Invite your students to share those stories. Help them see that emigrating to a new country presents challenges and that part of moving to a new culture entails learning how to adapt. You could label this sharing your "Pilgrim Project" so your students understand the concept of modern pilgrims.

• Ask your students why some of the children were calling Molly names, and what your students could do if they see such an occurrence in their school. Help your students see that cultural sensitivity is an important life skill and when they see someone being teased or bullied, they should take action and stand up for what is right. Have your class brainstorm appropriate things they could say or do if they witness such a situation.

• Ask your students to describe a time when they were newcomers and whether other students made them feel welcome. Also ask if they have ever found themselves in a situation similar to Molly's and how they responded. Then ask them to think of ways in which Molly could have tried to address her situation. Should she have just ignored the other girls, or should she have asserted herself by saying something to them or talking to her teacher? Help your students recognize that when someone says something unkind, it does not help to respond in the same way. Instead one needs to come up with an honest response to let the other person know how you feel. Perhaps Molly could have said, "Your name calling makes me feel uncomfortable."

• Elizabeth's comments to Molly reflect her insensitivity and her lack of understanding of cultural differences. Ask your students why this might be. Have your students work with a partner and role-play a conversation between Elizabeth and another classmate who attempts to help Elizabeth increase her understanding of Molly's situation and see how hurtful her comments have been. Point out that at first even Miss Stickley showed a lack of understanding and that adults as well as children can increase their cultural awareness.

- Discuss the reasons Molly's family left Russia. While they left for religious reasons, what are other reasons immigrants and refugees leave their countries? Encourage your immigrant and refugee students to share their personal experiences, and help raise your students' awareness and understanding of their plight.

Suggested Follow-up Activities

- This story lends itself to a discussion on bullying. Explain that when children are made to feel uncomfortable through name-calling, taunting, or exclusion, it is also considered bullying. Impress upon your students that if they are victims of or witnesses to such behavior, they should immediately seek an adult for help.
- Discuss ways Molly's classmates could have helped her feel welcome. (Suggestions might include taking an interest in her cultural background, finding out about her interests and hobbies, and including her in their activities.)

Transition Education Links

This story links with Chapter 4, "Personal and Cultural Identity." Miss Stickley refers to the Jewish religious celebration *Sukkoth* as having a similar cultural base to the American Thanksgiving. Ask your students to share information about their own religious holidays. Then chart some of the similarities such as food, music, purpose of the holiday, and special customs that many holidays have in common. Help your students recognize and appreciate the cultural diversity present in your classroom.

The story also links with Chapter 5, "Friendships and Relationships." Encourage your students to find ways to reach out to new students in your school community. Help your students prepare a "Welcome Book" in which they illustrate and write about the special holidays that are celebrated at your school. The book could be designed in a calendar fashion, starting with the first month of school and ending with summer vacation. This "Welcome Book" could then be given to new students from other countries who may not know a lot about the holidays in your country. Since many students may celebrate different holidays, it would help for the class first to brainstorm the important holidays that should be included.

Once your "Welcome Book" is complete, have the class brainstorm other ways in which new students could be helped to feel more at home in your school. In addition to being given a buddy to help them acclimate to your school, what other things could your class do that would make them feel welcome?

LESSON PLAN, GRADES K–5

The Lotus Seed
by Sherry Garland

Synopsis

This is the story of a Vietnamese woman who as a young girl had plucked one tiny lotus seed from a lotus pod in the emperor's Imperial Garden. She keeps this lotus seed with her always. One day, she has to flee Vietnam as a refugee and travel to America. She arrives as a widow and raises her children in America by working hard and saving her money. Many years later, her grandson discovers the lotus seed and buries it outside in the dirt, where it miraculously blooms the following spring.

Objectives

1. To provide students with the opportunity to explore ways to say good-bye when moving
2. To provide students with the opportunity to develop steps for effective decision making and problem solving
3. To provide students with the opportunity to learn ways to resolve conflicts and mend relationships

Activities Before Reading

• Ask students to think of one precious object or "treasure" that they own. Tell them to pretend that they are moving to a new country and can only choose one item to take with them when they move. Would they still pick the same treasured object? Give the students a slip of paper on which to write what that one object would be that they would carry with them to a new life in a new country. Have the students save their slips until after the story.

• Introduce the book by its cover, and explain that in this story they will meet a young girl who finds a treasured object of her own. Since the title gives the main clue about this object, ask your students to speculate why she chooses this object as her special treasure. Ask them to carefully listen to the story to find out what happens to that treasure.

Activities After Reading

• Ask the students about the significance of the lotus seed. Why was it so important to the grandmother? Help them understand that the lotus seed represented not only her homeland but everything her life had been before she became a refugee. It also represented the heritage and history of her people. Taking it with her made it somewhat easier for her to say good-bye to her homeland.

• The grandmother kept the lotus seed in a special place under the family altar. Ask your students if they have a special place in their home where they keep their own personal treasures. Ask them to share the treasured object they had written on the slip of paper and give a short explanation of its significance. How did they arrive at the decision to choose that item? Help them identify the thought process they went through. Did they consider what had the most meaning for them, what was most practical to take, or what was most unusual? Consider modeling this for them as you share a treasured object of your own.

• Explain to your students that when people leave their homeland or a special place they have lived, it helps to have an actual object to bring with them, something that is a tangible reminder of their life there. If it is not possible to bring something, writing about it can help them bring closure when they are leaving one part of their life and entering a new one. Ask your students to write about their special treasure in their journals. Have them describe the object, why they chose it, and whether they were actually able to bring it with them. Have them share their entries with partners or with the class. Respond to their entries in writing as well.

• Ask your students why the grandmother was so sad when her grandson buried the lotus seed and they could not find it. (She felt she had lost part of her cultural heritage.) When the lotus bloomed the next spring, however, the grandmother was given an even more special gift. Ask your students why the lotus seed became a never-ending gift. (The plant would continue to produce flowers from the seed from the homeland.)

• Share with your students the idea that sometimes we are forced to move, even when we do not want to. In this story the Vietnam War forced the grandmother to leave her homeland for a safer life somewhere else. Discuss other reasons that people leave their homelands, even if they are sad about doing so.

• The grandmother was devastated when she found out the seed was gone and could not be found. She cried, didn't eat, and didn't sleep. Discuss ways the grandson might try to mend his relationship with his grandmother. (He might comfort her, apologize for his actions, write her a note or poem, or bring her something to eat.) Ask your students to think of a conflict they have had with a brother, sister, friend, parent, or other adult. How did they resolve it, or how could they have resolved it? Encourage the children to share these experiences and chart the strategies they used.

Suggested Follow-up Activities

- This story provides an excellent opportunity to teach your students about the experience of being a refugee. Have them write a diary from the grandmother's point of view, reflecting her thoughts, feelings, and experiences once the war began, as she fled her country, and as she arrived in the new land. Invite your students to share these entries with the class. Discuss how these experiences compare to those of refugees today.
- Your students can create a mixed-media collage representing their homeland and the culture in which they are now living.

Transition Education Links

This story links with objectives in Chapter 2, "The Common Experience of Mobility." The lotus seed represented a powerful and special memory for the grandmother, and it therefore became her treasure. Invite students to bring in a special treasured object from home and share one special memory from a place where they have lived. Invite your students to also write a piece entitled "A Most Precious Memory I Have."

The lotus seed reminded the grandmother of the brave emperor and so she took it out whenever she felt sad or lonely. Ask your students if there is an object that brings them comfort when they are sad, lonely, or worried. Is it the same as or different from their special treasure?

This story also links with Chapter 3, "The Process of Transition." Even though the characters in this story were being forced to move and become refugees, they still went through the process of transition. Explore these stages with your students, and discuss how they might be the same or different for people who are forced to leave their country under difficult circumstances and at short notice.

It also provides an opportunity to discuss the experience of culture shock the grandmother had upon arriving in the United States. "She arrived in a strange new land with blinking lights and speeding cars and towering buildings that scraped the sky and a language she didn't understand." Using this quote as a basis for comparison have your students relate their own experiences when they arrived in a new place to the grandmother's.

This story also links with Chapter 4, "Personal and Cultural Identity." After the lotus plant bloomed, the grandmother gave each of her grandchildren a seed to remember her by. Her granddaughter plans to pass it on to her children one day, in this way sharing the history of her country and keeping her cultural heritage alive. Ask, "How do you keep your cultural heritage alive? Have you been given a special object by a relative in your family or a friend or neighbor from another place you lived?"

IDEAS FOR CROSS-CURRICULAR CONNECTIONS

Creative and Performing Arts

Have your students work on a small-group project to design a board game about moving. Have them use what they know about adjusting to a new place to include the benefits and challenges, and experiences a person might have. After the games are completed, provide time for the children to play them.

Have your students work together to plan and host an International Music Festival for your class. They may choose to learn to play different instruments or perform songs from their countries or cultures.

Social Studies

Consider teaching problem solving through topics studied in history. If you teach a unit on immigration, then give your students real life problems to solve. For example, if immigrants are allowed only one suitcase each to hold everything they will need for their trip to their new home, which items would be the most important to pack and why? Extend that idea by having your students first answer the question about immigrants of the past, and then have them consider the items contemporary immigrants would bring. How would those suitcases differ from one time period to another? What would you bring with you today? What would you have brought 50 years ago?

Research natural disasters that have occurred in recent history. How have people joined together to solve the problems involved and coped with floods, earthquakes, droughts, and brush fires?

Science

When their natural habitat is changed due to some natural phenomenon, some species will adapt to their environment. Adaptation is nature's way of problem solving to ensure the continuation of the species. For example, animals that live in areas of the world where there are extremes in climate will change or adapt to the different seasons. An arctic wolf will grow a heavy coat of fur to help withstand the severe arctic winter, but will shed this heavy coat for a lighter one during the arctic summer. Take a look with your students at areas of the world where animals have had to adapt to solve the problem of survival. Think in terms of deserts, tundra, rain forests, and so on.

Learn about the physical effects of worry and stress that can be associated with a move, and help your students explore ways to ease them. You may teach them relaxation techniques and breathing exercises as ways to reduce stress.

Math

Help your students figure out the time in different time zones of the world. The International Date Line is located in Greenwich, England, and all time zones are calculated from that point. When it is 9:00 a.m. in Greenwich, what time would it be in Beijing, China, and Lima, Peru? Display a world map, and draw in the time zones to help students with this abstract concept. Discuss situations where you might need to know the time in another part of the world. It could be calculating the time to phone a grandparent living in another country, or the time your plane will arrive when you visit there. Your students can write their own word problems to illustrate these situations.

Chapter 7

Moving Back

Although children who move domestically may return to a place they have lived before, this chapter is primarily aimed at children who move back from abroad where the cultural and language differences are more significant. If you have students in your class who are getting ready to move back home, you can help them prepare for the transition and know what to expect. Conversely, if you are receiving students who are returning home after living abroad, your understanding of the issues they may be facing can help their readjustment tremendously.

Most families who move abroad do eventually return to live in their home countries. While some return to a different city, state, or region than before, some return to the same city and possibly the same house they left. Moving back to a city, state, or country where one has lived before is perhaps the most difficult transition of all. There are three reasons for this:

1. We usually don't anticipate the need for adjustment when returning home. We expect to fit in and others expect us to as well. In actual fact, we experience adjustment issues similar to those when we moved abroad.

2. We are unaware of how much we have changed until we return home. It is often not until we are living back in our own country that we realize how our awareness, attitudes, knowledge, and values now differ from others in our own culture and from family and friends we left behind.

3. We all have particular expectations of "home," and we are disappointed when they are not met. Most people think of "home" as a place that is familiar, and where they feel completely comfortable and have a sense of belonging. Yet upon their return they find that people, places, and ways of doing things such as purchasing groceries may have changed. Somehow we seem to expect time to have stood still while we were away.

It is important to recognize that for many children, moving to their passport country is not really moving "back," but in fact may be the first time they will live there. Their knowledge of their passport country is largely derived from their visits home, and their parents' stories and recollections of home, but this "home" is actually their parents' "home." For many children, moving to their passport country is like moving to another foreign country, and their adjustment process may best be approached that way. Children who have grown up in a different country often have a different sense of "home" than their parents. Many friends, family members, and teachers make the mistake of expecting children to know the culture of a place when they have never lived there or have lived away for a long time. Some of your students may have a passport from more than one country and possibly from a country other than their parents.

People also go through the process of transition (see Chapter 3) when moving back home. There will be things they are excited about and others they are sad to leave behind. As with the cultural adjustment experienced when moving to a new place, there are predictable stages to moving back, or reentry adjustment. This usually includes a brief *honeymoon period*, the disorientation of *reverse culture shock,* and finally *readjustment*. It is important to remember, however, that we all respond to change differently and no one will have exactly the same experience. The response to reentry is also individual regardless of age.

There are many variables that affect the way people experience the process of reentry adjustment. Some of these variables are the amount of time spent abroad; how they felt about the place they lived; the extent to which they were immersed in the culture of the place; how different the culture was; the degree of contact they had with their home while they were away; whether the move back was expected or unexpected, voluntary or involuntary; and the amount of notice time they had prior to moving back. It is useful to talk with your students about the reasons people move back home. These include a parent's job, elderly or ailing relatives, the health needs of a family member, educational opportunities, and the parents' desire for their children to experience living in their own culture. A child's response to moving back will also be influenced by his or her own personality and the parents' response to the move.

As we have mentioned throughout this book, children need opportunities to share their experiences. Find opportunities for your students to incorporate into class projects the knowledge and skills they have acquired living elsewhere. This gives them an authentic way to share the interesting experiences they have had and the knowledge and skills they have gained. It is an enormous comfort for children to know that who they are and what they know is valued. This kind of sharing presents a wonderful opportunity for students to see that they can learn from each other and to value what others may have to teach them. You are a powerful role model and when children see that you value and respect the backgrounds and experiences of others, they will see them as important as well.

find they don't have that much in common anymore. Encourage children to develop new friendships as well as nurture old ones.

5. *Some people including family and friends may be uninterested in our experiences*. Most people returning home are brimming with stories to tell and experiences to share. It is a common experience that family and friends show little interest in hearing about our past experiences when we return for a visit or move back home. While this can be quite hurtful and disappointing, it is helpful to understand why this happens. It is not that others do not care about us; often it is simply hard for them to relate to our experiences, particularly experiences we have had abroad, and they may even feel a twinge of envy. It is important to talk with children about showing interest in the experiences of others as well. As we reestablish relationships, we will find opportunities to be able to share more about ourselves and our past experiences.

6. *Reentry adjustment and reverse culture shock are experiences of moving back*. Even though we are moving back to a country and culture we know, we go through a process of readjustment. Initially there is usually a *honeymoon period* where we are happy to be back in our own country, and we do all the things we missed while we were away. There are often parties to welcome us home, and we frequent favorite restaurants, go to favorite places, and visit friends and family. Once the excitement wears off and we become immersed in every day life, we usually experience some degree of *reverse culture shock*. We may feel disoriented by sights, sounds, smells, and routines that are no longer familiar, and we may feel out of step with our peers. Finally, we become involved with friends, family, and activities again. Life becomes more familiar, and we experience some degree of *readjustment* to life back in our own culture.

7. *Effective strategies for readjusting to moving back can be developed*. Most of the skills for adjusting to a new location can be used to address the challenges of moving back home. It is most important for children to have realistic expectations and know that living in their own country will be different than when they lived there before. Help them realize that it will probably take time to readjust to life in their own country. They may feel out of step with their friends and peers at first while they are learning about current trends and rediscovering the ways things are done. See Appendix E, "Approaches to Transition," and Appendix F, "Tips for Parents," for suggested strategies.

8. *The knowledge and skills acquired from living in a new place can be useful when moving back*. Some of the skills acquired when living abroad include learning to make new friends, reading maps to find one's way around, learning a new language, or learning about different places and cultures. Children can use these skills to make new friends back home, find out about their new neighborhood, share in school projects, and communicate with

others who speak the language they have learned. You can have a positive role in helping your students know themselves and explore ways they can use the skills, knowledge, attitudes, and awareness they have acquired while living elsewhere.

Objectives: To provide students with the opportunity

- to discuss their concerns about returning to their home neighborhood, city, state, or country
- to learn about and discuss the common experiences of moving back
- to explore ways they have changed as a result of living abroad or in another place
- to learn about reentry adjustment and reverse culture shock
- to develop effective strategies to address the challenges of moving back
- to find ways to reestablish relationships with their family and peers
- to identify the knowledge, skills, attitudes, and awareness they bring back with them and how they can be used

LESSON PLAN, GRADES K–5

When Africa Was Home
by Karen Lynn Williams

Synopsis

Peter is a young boy who is growing up in Africa while his father is working there. Peter loves living in his African village and relishes the life he has always known there. When the father's work is finished, the family moves back to America, but Peter considers Africa his real home. Peter has difficulty adjusting to life in America, and the family all miss Africa very much. His father's work eventually brings them back to Africa, much to Peter's delight. Once Peter is reunited with his African nanny and friends, he resumes the African life he had grown to love.

Objectives

1. To provide students with the opportunity to discuss their concerns about moving back to their passport country
2. To provide students with the opportunity to learn about and discuss the common experiences of moving back

3. To provide students with the opportunity to develop strategies to address the challenges of moving back
4. To provide students with the opportunity to learn about reentry adjustment and reverse culture shock
5. To provide students with the opportunity to identify the knowledge, skills, attitudes, and awareness they bring back with them and how they can be used

Activities Before Reading

• Write the word *memories* on the board and ask your students for a definition. They will most likely say that memories are people or events or experiences that stand out in your mind; ones that you remember throughout the years. Memories are often associated with the five senses: taste, touch, sight, sound, and smell. Share with your students one "sense memory" that you have from a place where you have lived. This could be a place from your childhood. It might be the crunch of autumn leaves under your feet as you walked home from school, or the voice of a trolley conductor as he called out the names of the stops along your route. Then ask your students to think of one such "sense memory" from a place where they have lived. Tell your students that this story describes the "sense memories" of a boy who moves back to America after growing up in Africa.

Activities After Reading

• Peter did not want to leave Africa and return to the United States. For him, Africa was home because he grew up there. Explain that sometimes children have a different idea of where "home" is than their parents. The concept of "home," however, is most likely the place where you felt you most belonged, even if it wasn't your passport country. This can happen even when it is not your parents' country of birth. Reassure your students this is perfectly natural, especially if you have lived a long time in another country. Some people actually feel at home in more than one location, country, or culture.

• For some children, moving back may actually be moving back to their parent's home country, and it may be the first time they are living there. This was Peter's experience. Help your students identify some of the concerns Peter had about moving back to America. (Peter was worried that he wouldn't have the words he would need or that he wouldn't be able to sleep without the mosquito net tucked all around him.) Explain that it is natural to have concerns when moving, even if you are moving back to a place you lived before. What could Peter have done to ease his worries?

Invite your students to share their concerns and discuss ways they can address them. (These may include talking with their parents or finding out more about the place they will live.)

• Peter had to adjust to different customs. No one asked how he slept, and people "talked funny" in America. Ask your students if there is anything that surprised them about adjusting to living back in their own country or the last time they visited there. Was there anything they found difficult? Explain that sometimes our home country can feel unfamiliar when we have lived in a different culture and known a different way of life. It may take time to adjust to living back in our own culture.

• You can teach older students about the experience of culture shock and reverse culture shock. Have the children work in pairs to examine the text of the story and compile a list of the new experiences Peter had when he moved back to America. (The list might include flying in an airplane, seeing big-city lights, experiencing winter and snow, wearing winter clothes, watching television, seeing a vacuum cleaner, and eating different foods like popsicles and pizza.) Explain that sometimes things in our own country may seem unfamiliar when we have lived in a different place for a time and that this feeling of disorientation and the sense that we don't belong is part of reverse culture shock. Ask your students to share their own experiences of reverse culture shock, which is often similar to the culture shock they may have experienced when they moved away from home.

• Peter does not feel like he belongs in America. Have you ever felt like you did not belong somewhere? What helped you fit in or feel more at home in a place? What are some things that might have made Peter feel better about being in America? (Some suggestions might include making new friends, meeting other African children, or decorating his room with African art or posters to remind him of an important part of his life.)

• Have your students help you compile a list of the "sense memories" that Peter had of living in Africa. It might include:

Brightly colored clothing
Tall anthills
Maize fields
Chattering of monkeys
Taste of corn paste and sugarcane
Touch of mosquito netting on his bed
Sound of drums in the distance
Big, bright stars

• Talk with your students about Peter's move back to America. Why was he unhappy when he arrived back in America? (He missed his African way of life.) What did he miss about Africa? (Peter likely missed the warm rains of Africa, his *mayi's* warm corn paste, his *mayi* and Yekha, the feel of the warm earth under his feet, and the sweet taste of sugarcane.) Have your students describe the people and places they miss from other places they have lived, and give them an opportunity to reminisce.

    • While his family could not bring things like the anthills back to America, what might have helped Peter's transition to a new way of life? (Perhaps they could have helped him learn more about America, brought a special object such as kente cloth or a small African drum to keep in his room, or taken photographs of him with his *mayi* and Yekha, his village, and the African animals.) Was there an African dish they might still be able to prepare to help Peter feel connected to the African part of his life? Point out that when we have lived in more than one culture, we take parts of those cultures with us wherever else we may live—even when we move back home. Sometimes we do not have choices about moving, but we can bring parts of our favorite cultures to wherever we make our new home. Often our favorite parts of other cultures linger in our memories all our lives. Discuss things your students could do if they are moving back.

    • Peter has an awareness and understanding of African culture from having lived there. He understands the language, knows the customs and foods, and has a great deal of knowledge about daily life. How could he share that knowledge with other people in America? (Perhaps he could teach his classmates about Africa, show them games he played there, share foods he ate, and tell them about animals that live there.) Provide an opportunity for your students to share their knowledge of places they have lived.

Suggested Follow-up Activities

    • Children who are moving back to their passport country or to another country can write their own book entitled *When ——— Was Home*.

    • Give your students an opportunity to create their own "memory passports." Take paper and fold it into a book with at least six pages. On the front have the students write their name and the name of their passport country. On the following pages ask them to write the names of countries or places they have lived, and on each page have them write or draw a special "sense memory" about that place. Once the books are finished, give students an opportunity to share them.

Transition Education Links

    This story has links with Chapter 2, "The Common Experience of Mobility." Africa was "home" for Peter. Help your students explore the meaning of "home" and identify where "home" is for them. Using the African word *kwatu* from the end of the story, have the children draw or write about their *kwatu* or home.

This story links with Chapter 3, "The Process of Transition." It is clear that Peter does not want to leave Africa. This has been the only home he has ever known. Explain that everyone responds differently to the experiences of moving and of moving back home. Usually there are not only things to look forward to, but things to miss as well. Discuss the responses your students had to hearing they were moving back.

You may want to give your students a personal opportunity to express how they feel about a special place they lived and the grief and sense of loss in having to move away. Give them a sheet of paper with the title, "Ten Things I Loved Best about Living in _____." Have them fill in the 10 items and then invite them to a writer's conference with you. Give them time to talk about those things that were so special and encourage them to write about them.

Teach your students about the process of transition by explaining the different stages of the ADAPT model. Help them identify the stages Peter experienced. He experienced the "All is well" stage (Involvement Stage), the "Don't want to go, or do I?" stage (Leaving Stage), and the "Anything is possible!" stage (Transition Stage). Point out that Peter remained in the Transition Stage and never moved into the "Perhaps this isn't so bad" stage (Entering Stage). Instead he waited for the day he could return to Africa. Discuss ways he could have entered into life in America and enjoyed it during the time he was there.

This story also links with Chapter 4, "Personal and Cultural Identity." Provide an opportunity for your students to share their cultural backgrounds and the knowledge of other cultures they have experienced. Have your students create their own books showing the similarities and differences between life in their passport country and the country in which they lived before. You might use the book, *A Country Far Away* (1988) by Nigel Gray, which contrasts the life of a boy in Africa with a British child as a model.

Peter's life was deeply influenced by his *mayi* (nanny), and his best friend, Yekha. Help your students to identify the cultural influences of other people in their lives in the places they have lived.

This story has links with Chapter 5, "Friendships and Relationships" as well. Peter had "two mothers" in Africa and had a special relationship with his *mayi*, and his friend, Yehka. Explore the different kinds of relationships your students may have had with other members of the community in places they have lived. Help them to identify the ways their friendships with children and adults of other cultures have enriched their lives.

Ask your students to describe cultural practices they have learned from friends or neighbors, or from traveling to or living in a different place. Are there cultural practices they still include in their daily lives?

LESSON PLAN, GRADES K–5

Tea With Milk
by Allen Say

Synopsis

May is a young Japanese girl who has lived all her life in America. After she graduates from high school, her parents decide to return to Japan, the country of their birth. May is uncomfortable living in Japan because she is used to the way of life in California, and Japan feels like a foreign country to her. At first she is very unhappy, but May eventually begins to adapt to her new life in Japan. She finds a way to use the skills and attitudes she learned while living in America to blend her American ways with her Japanese culture and find happiness living in Japan. This is the true story of the author's mother.

Objectives

1. To provide students with the opportunity to learn about and discuss the common experiences of moving back
2. To provide students with the opportunity to explore ways they have changed as a result of living abroad or in another place
3. To provide students with the opportunity to learn about reentry adjustment and reverse culture shock
4. To provide students with the opportunity to develop strategies to address the challenges of moving back
5. To provide students with the opportunity to identify the knowledge, skills, attitudes, and awareness they bring back with them and how they can be used

Activities Before Reading

• Draw a "Sequence Triangle" on the board by drawing a very large equilateral triangle. Draw a large circle on the tip of each point. Label the top circle of the triangle "Passport Country." Move down to the circle on the bottom right of the triangle and label it "New Country." Label the final circle "Permanent Changes." Explain to your students that as people move from their passport country to a new country they bring certain customs with them. Once they have lived in a new country, some of their customs may change as they adapt to the new customs of the country in which they live. When we move back home we are changed to some degree because of the new ideas, customs, and language we have learned while living abroad. Explain to your class that the Sequence Triangle represents one's life abroad. It describes the experiences a person has when he or she moves from one culture to another, carrying cultural changes with him or her on each subsequent move. Explain that this story describes the changes a young Japanese woman experiences when she moves to Japan for the first time.

Activities After Reading

- Refer to the Sequence Triangle. Ask the class where May's passport country would be. America is the answer, although Japan is her parents' passport country. Make sure your students understand the difference. Write "America" in the top circle. Then ask the students where May moved. Since Japan is the answer, write "Japan" in the bottom right-hand circle. In the last circle write May's two names: her American name, "May," and her Japanese name, "Masako."
- Then as a class, complete the rest of the Sequence Triangle. This is done by writing on the outer lines of the triangle. On the right sideline list the American cultural customs that May had adopted while being raised in California. These might include the type of clothing May wore in America and some of her favorite foods. Make sure to also include how she drank her tea with milk and sugar. On the bottom line connecting the bottom right circle to the bottom left circle, ask the class about some of the foods that she now ate in Japan, the type of clothing she wore there, and the traditional classes she attended.
- On the final line, ask your students for examples of some of the customs that May adopted and the skills she learned from both cultures that helped her to succeed in her new life. May spoke both Japanese and English, was independent and assertive, and learned some of the traditional Japanese skills such as calligraphy, flower arranging, and how to perform a tea ceremony. The title of this book, *Tea with Milk*, represents how May retained this Western custom throughout her life.
- Once the entire Sequence Triangle is filled in, initiate a discussion with your students about how people change due to their life experiences. People who have lived in a different culture usually adopt some of the customs and behaviors.

- Finally, give your students an opportunity to develop their own Sequence Triangle. Have them write their passport country or the place where they were born in the top circle. Then have them choose the country they are living in now or another country where they have lived, and label the second circle. Their name, including their passport name and adopted name if they have one, goes in the final circle. Young children can write simple experiences from one line to the next, like greetings given in the passport country and new greetings they learned abroad. The last line can list their favorite greetings. Older students can include several ideas on each line such as new games, new vocabulary, new clothing, and new customs they learned. Once all the Sequence Triangles are complete, give students an opportunity to share their individual Sequence Triangle with the class. Encourage them to reflect on how they have changed as a result of living abroad or in different places within the same country.

- When May arrived in Japan, she had difficulty adjusting to life there. She missed the foods she ate and the way of life in California. She felt like she didn't belong, and other children called her a stranger. Explain to your students that sometimes when we move back we feel like we don't fit in because the way of life in our own culture has become unfamiliar. This is often surprising because this is the place we are supposed to fit in and other people expect us to know the culture. Although May was Japanese she did not know all of the traditions in Japan and had to learn some of them. Invite your students who have moved back to share their experiences. Tell your students about some of the other common experiences people have when moving back. Point out that some of these are similar to the experiences they may have had when they first moved away.

- May had to repeat a year in school because her educational experiences had been different than if she had lived in Japan. Explain that children often find that their experience in school is different from country to country. Encourage them to ask questions if there is something they do not know or understand.

- When May arrived in Japan, her surroundings looked unfamiliar and some of the customs were new to her. Explain that this feeling of disorientation and the sense that one doesn't belong are experiences of reverse culture shock. Have your students who have moved back describe their experiences of reverse culture shock. Point out that it takes time to readjust to your own culture when you have been living in a different one.

- In order to adjust to life in Japan, May talked with her parents about her thoughts and feelings; she learned some of the traditions of her own culture; she eventually found a way to use the skills she had in her life in Japan; and she made a friend with similar background experiences. What are some other strategies that might have helped? Perhaps her parents could have helped her know what to expect in her new life there. Explore other strategies your students could use to adjust to living back home. Help your students determine what they would like to know about the place they are moving to, and explore ways to help them find that information.

• When May lived in California, she had rice, miso, and green tea for breakfast at home, and pancakes and muffins at her friends' houses. She was able to move back and forth between her home culture and that of her friends. Later in Japan she continued to adjust to Japanese and Western cultural situations. Discuss the reasons why the ability to adapt to different cultures is a valuable life skill. Ask your students to describe situations in their lives where they adapt to different cultural situations. How is this skill useful to them? How can it be used in new situations?

• Invite your students who have moved back or are getting ready to move back to describe the skills they have learned living abroad. Help them find ways they can use them back in their passport country. Consider providing an opportunity for them to teach the class a poem in a different language or share traditions they learned about in another culture.

Suggested Follow-up Activities

• Parents may expect their children to adopt the traditions of the passport culture, while children may have new ideas and resist adopting the "old ways." Ask your students to point out some of the clashes between May and her parents. At first, the clashes deal with clothing, food, and schooling. Eventually when her parents wanted to arrange her marriage and have her lead the life of a traditional Japanese housewife, May rebelled. Why was May unhappy? (She had learned to be more independent while living in America.) Could a compromise have been reached between her and her parents? Why was May happier when she moved to the city of Osaka?

• Initiate a discussion with your class about having realistic expectations. Life back home does not always meet our expectations because people and situations have changed. Talk with your students about why this occurs and how we sometimes have an idea in our mind of how something will be. Discuss with your class possible changes that can occur while living away from your passport country. Friends may have moved on, teachers may have retired, or shopkeepers may have sold out to developers. Life is never exactly the same, but at the same time we ourselves have changed too. Explain that by having realistic expectations the process of moving back can be eased.

Transition Education Links

This story links with Chapter 2, "The Common Experience of Mobility." May's future husband says, "Home isn't a place or a building that's ready made and waiting for you in America or anywhere" (p. 30). Discuss this idea with your students, and give them the opportunity to explore what "home" means to them and where they consider "home."

There are also links with Chapter 4, "Personal and Cultural Identity." Discuss how torn May feels because she identifies so strongly with the American culture, while her parents identify more strongly with the Japanese culture. Once she found a way to express both parts of herself, wearing the kimono no longer seemed uncomfortable. Help your students gain an awareness of their cultural or multicultural identity. Discuss the ways your students express their multicultural selves.

LESSON PLAN, GRADES K–5

Going Home
by Eve Bunting

Synopsis

Carlos and his family live in the United States, where his parents are farmworkers. It is almost Christmas, and he and his family are going home to visit Mexico. While his parents are excited about the trip, Carlos and his sisters are not so sure about it. Although they were born there, Mexico does not feel like their home. Once they see their relatives again and their parents' joy at returning to their village, they begin to understand that Mexico can be home as well. While this story is not about returning home to live, it lends itself to discussing many of the experiences children have when moving back to their passport country.

Objectives

1. To provide students with the opportunity to discuss their concerns about moving back home
2. To provide students with the opportunity to learn about and discuss the common experiences of moving back
3. To provide students with the opportunity to learn about the process of reentry adjustment and reverse culture shock

4. To provide students with the opportunity to discuss ways to reestablish relationships with family when they move back

Activities Before Reading

• Write the word *opportunity* on the board and ask your students to give
you a definition. After several students have shared their thoughts, brainstorm with the class different types of opportunities that exist. (There are
opportunities for a good education, for a career, for travel, for making new
friends, and so on.) Then ask them if there are certain attitudes that insure
you can take advantage of an opportunity. (Some attitudes might be to have
an open mind and to be flexible to accept what an opportunity might offer.)
• Now write the word *choice* on the board and ask your students for
a definition. Then ask them how the term *choice* fits in with the concept of
"opportunity." Explain that everyone is given choices in life, and it is the
choices we make that affect our opportunities. Tell them to listen carefully
to the story so they can understand the choices the characters made.

Activities After Reading

• Carlos and his sisters were not so sure about going to Mexico. Ask
your students why they think the children felt this way. Possible answers
might be that they did not know what Mexico would be like or what their
family there were like. Explain that, for some children, moving back to their
passport country doesn't quite feel like moving home because they have
grown up living someplace else. It may feel like home to their parents, but
not to them. Like the children in the story, they may hardly remember it.
Have your students write or draw about what they remember about their
home country. Give them the opportunity to voice their concerns about
moving back. Explain that people often worry about fitting in and what
the new place will be like. Discuss many of the common experiences of
moving back.
• At one point in the story Mama says that home is both in Mexico
and in America. Ask your students if that is possible. Is it possible to have
two homes, the one where you are from and the one where you are living
now? Then ask students to draw a large heart on a piece of paper and divide it in half. Have them put the things they love best about their current
home on the left side of the heart and the things that they love best about
their original home on the right side of the heart. Invite your students to
share these with each other.
• As the family drives through Mexico, they see many traditional sights.
List these with your students. (They include flowers hanging from lampposts;

streets of smooth, shiny stones; men and women on bicycles; an old man leading a burro piled high with firewood; and sheep in the road.) These sights are probably unfamiliar to the children, as they have not lived in Mexico for a long time. Explain that moving back home may seem unfamiliar if you have been away for a long time, and that it will take time to get used to it again. Use this opportunity to teach older children more about the experience of reentry adjustment and the stages of reverse culture shock. Encourage your students who have moved back to describe their experiences readjusting to living in their passport country.

• Explain that when we have lived away from our family and friends, it often takes time to get closer to them again. It has been a long time since the children in the story have seen their Mexican neighbors and relatives. Discuss ways they can reach out and get to know them better. Perhaps they can ask questions about their lives, take part in their daily activities, try to speak to them in Spanish, and tell them about their lives in America. Talk with your students about ways they can reestablish closer relationships with the special people in their lives now that they are living back home. Remind them that it is important to show an interest in the lives of others and to share their experiences a bit at a time.

• Home usually has special meaning, especially in the memory of the person who has had to leave it behind. Help your students create some cinquain poems about their memories of their home country. Start by having them brainstorm words that describe the physical attributes of their home. Then have them list words that would describe emotional attributes of their home. Cinquain poems follow this format:

Line 1 has one word that names the subject (*Home*).
Line 2 has two words that describe the subject (*Brick, wood*).
Line 3 has three words that describe some action (*Eating, sleeping, talking*) related to the subject.
Line 4 has a short phrase about the subject (*Where I feel safe*).
Line 5 contains one word that is synonymous with the subject (*Soul*).
Another example is:
Mexico
Bright, colorful
Talking, laughing, remembering
Where I was born
Home

• Follow this activity by discussing the expectations people usually have when moving back. We often have an idea of what "home" will be like from our memories of that place. Most likely people and situations will have changed. Have your students list the hopes and expectations they have for when they arrive back home. Help them identify the situations that may have changed and to have realistic expectations.

• The children witness a tender moment when their parents dance in the moonlight, and they realize how much their parents love their country. Explain that for some children "home" may feel like a different place, but they can try to understand their parents' love of their country and take pride in their own cultural heritage. Help them to explore ways they can find a place for themselves in their "home" country. Let them know that home can become "home" again.

Suggested Follow-up Activities

• Through your class discussions help your students understand that parents often make sacrifices in their own lives so that their children will have better opportunities than they did. In this story the parents' most obvious sacrifice was leaving Mexico, but there were other sacrifices as well. Ask your students to think about possible sacrifices their parents have made in order to provide a better life for them and their family. Then suggest that your students write a special thank-you note to their parents for specific sacrifices that were made in order to ensure they had positive opportunities.

• Have your students draw sights and sounds they remember from their home country. Compare them with the sights and sounds of the country they just left or the one they live in now and are getting ready to leave.

Transition Education Links

This story has links with objectives in Chapter 2, "The Common Experience of Mobility." As they are leaving for Mexico, Mother hugs Carlos. "Home is here," she says. "But it is there, too." Have your students explore the concept of "home" and determine where "home" is for them. Discuss the idea of whether "home" can be more than one place, and if so, how?

There are also links with Chapter 4, "Personal and Cultural Identity." Carlos and his sisters have grown up in the United States and hardly remember Mexico. Unlike their parents, they have learned English and have been exposed to the American culture at school. Children may relate to the lifestyle in the country they are living in and know little about their own passport country. Encourage children to see the value of knowing their own culture as well, and help them celebrate their multicultural selves.

LESSON PLAN, GRADES K–5

The Trip Back Home
by Janet S. Wong

Synopsis

A young girl and her mother prepare for a visit "back home" to the village in Korea where her mother was raised. The mother and daughter choose thoughtful gifts from America to bring to their Korean relatives. Once the mother and daughter arrive in Korea, they share in the Korean lifestyle of their family and create special memories together. When they get ready to return to America, they delight in the gifts their Korean family gives them as mementos of "back home." This story is based on the author's childhood experiences.

Objectives

1. To provide students with the opportunity to find ways to reestablish relationships with their family and friends
2. To provide students with the opportunity to identify the knowledge, skills, attitudes, and awareness they bring back with them and how they can be used

Activities Before Reading

• Ask your students to list the names of family members and friends "back home" and the activities they usually enjoy doing with them. Have them also make a gift list with ideas for special gifts they might bring them. For example, Aunt Susie may love to golf and therefore a special gift might be a golf towel from St. Andrews in Scotland. Explain that in this story a child and her mother exchange special gifts with their family and also share in their lives during a visit to Korea.

Activities After Reading

• Ask your students to think about the three gifts that the little girl and her mother chose to take as presents to Korea. Why do you think they selected those gifts? How can we choose gifts for others that are meaningful?
• Discuss how the hugs the girl and her mother received in return were also special gifts. Talk about gifts we can give and receive that are

intangible, but so special. Some of those gifts are the caring, love, and support we show toward others.

- Have your students think of some of the "gifts" they have been given as a result of living in a different country or place. These might include speaking a new language, learning a new custom, and the opportunity to travel to different places. Ask your students to think of other intangible gifts they have received as a result of living abroad and help them see that some of these gifts are skills and knowledge. Discuss ways they can use these wherever they go.
- In this story the little girl eats traditional Korean foods while she is visiting her relatives. Ask your class to make a list of the different foods they have experienced eating from places they have lived or visited. Are there foods that they would like to continue enjoying after they move "back home"?
- Once the mother and daughter arrive in Korea, they eagerly participate in their relatives' lives. The child fed the pigs, and with her relatives, shopped at the market, prepared meals, stored the persimmons, sewed clothes, told stories, and played cards. In this way she became closer to her family. Point out that one way to reestablish relationships with our family and friends is to show an interest in their lives, particularly after we have lived apart.

Suggested Follow-up Activities

- A dragon kite is used at both the beginning and the end of this story. Have your students design their own paper kites with artwork symbolic of the places they have lived before moving home as their own memento.
- Have your students create acrostic poems about their passport country or another country in which they have lived. In an acrostic poem you write each letter of the name of the country down the left side of the paper. For each letter the student must then come up with a phrase or sentence that describes something about the country or is a special memory.
One example is given here:

K—kites are flying in the sky in springtime
O—oil is used to stir-fry vegetables
R—rice cakes can be bought in the marketplace
E—egg scraps are fed to the pigs
A—autumn is when the persimmons are stored

Transition Education Links

This story has links with Chapter 6, "Problem-Solving Skills." The mother and child had to decide what gifts they could bring to Korea from America that would be meaningful. Moving back home necessitates that children, as well as their parents, have to make choices about the items they will carry back home with them from the country or place in which they have been living. Have your students decide which items they would bring and explain why.

LESSON PLAN, GRADES K–5

"They Don't Do Math in Texas" (In *If You're Not Here, Please Raise Your Hand*) by Kalli Dakos

Synopsis

In this poem a student describes how Kate, a new student, keeps talking about how wonderful life was when she lived in Texas. As the poem continues, the reader begins to sense how annoyed the other students are with the supposed glories of her school in Texas compared to their school.

Objectives

1. To provide students with the opportunity to discuss their concerns about returning to their home neighborhood, city, state, or country
2. To provide students with the opportunity to learn about and discuss the common experiences of moving back
3. To provide students with the opportunity to develop strategies to address the challenges of moving back
4. To provide students with the opportunity to find ways to reestablish relationships with their family and peers

Activities Before Reading

• Ask your students to give you a definition for the word *bragging*, and have them discuss the reasons they think people brag. (Sometimes people brag to make themselves feel more important or to bring attention to themselves so that they will "fit in.") During the discussion make sure you point out that not everyone who brags is aware that they are bragging.

Sometimes people are so proud of information and knowledge they have learned that they do not realize they are sharing it inappropriately. Also point out that sometimes it is not *what* you say but *how* you say something that makes it sound like bragging.

  • Tell your students to listen to the following poem about a girl named Kate and try to figure out why she is bragging about Texas.

Activities After Reading

  • Tell your students that while Kalli Dakos wrote this poem with humor, there are several important underlying issues to explore. Discuss the reasons Kate might have been bragging about and exaggerating her life in Texas. Perhaps she felt lonely and missed her old school and life in Texas. Explain that these are common experiences people have when they move, whether it is to another location or back home. Ask your students to share other experiences they have had.

  • Discuss ways your students can approach or address the challenges of moving back. Some suggestions might be to be patient and know it takes time, talk with their parents about their feelings, find ways to do what they like back home, reach out and make new friends, explore and get to know the new place, or rediscover their home community.

  • Have the students look at Stanza 2 where Kate says she was in sixth grade in Texas, instead of fourth grade. Ask students to think back to a previous school they attended and ask them what academic challenges or differences existed when they came to their present school. Explain that schools all over the world are different and it is natural to have some adjustments.

Explain how it can be very different if you move from the Southern Hemisphere to the Northern Hemisphere or vice versa. When it is summer in the northern hemisphere it is winter in the southern one. So what happens when a student moves from Argentina to England in the month of December? That would be in the middle of summer vacation in Argentina and the end of one school year, but in the middle of a school year in England.

  • In what ways could the students in Kate's new school help her feel more a part of the class and at the same time validate her feelings about Texas? One idea might be for them to ask her to bring in a photo album or yearbook from her old school to share with the class. It is important to talk with your students about showing interest in others when they move back home or to a new place.

  • Why does Kate say, "In Texas I was pure gold, while here I'm just another rock?" (p. 19) Help your students realize that when they move they may feel like Kate until people get to know them and they feel like part of their community again. Brainstorm ways in which your class can make newcomers feel welcome and can show an interest in new students and their previous experiences.

• Talk with your class about some of the harder elements of moving and leaving a school where they were happy. Leaving friends is perhaps the hardest part, but leaving familiar routines and teachers they felt comfortable with is also difficult. Invite your students to share the concerns they have about moving, particularly moving back.

• Draw attention to the last part of the poem where the speaker says he hopes Kate learns to like their school before everyone hates her. Explain that hate is a really strong term and that in this poem Kate was certainly annoying, but not really hateful. Now ask your students to think of helpful suggestions they could give to Kate on how she could share about her life in Texas without bragging about it.

Suggested Follow-up Activities

• This poem lends itself to dramatic reading or role-playing. Pair students and have them take on the two roles of Kate and the speaker. Then ask one of the pairs to perform their read aloud in front of the class. Again, have the class pay attention to how the message about Texas was delivered. Take one of the stanzas and ask the students to read it in a different voice—one without bragging—and see if the message comes across in a different manner.

• Have students write their own scenario of a new student moving into their community and how they might talk on and on about their old school and where they used to live. Discuss how that student could have shared information in a more appropriate way. Have your students then write a dialogue where both children show an interest in and learn about each other. Explain that this is an important skill in building positive relationships with other people.

• Point out that sometimes when people move back home, their friends and family show little interest in their experiences living abroad. This is usually because it is hard for them to relate to what it was like. Sometimes the way we talk about our experiences can also seem like bragging. Suggest that children share a little at a time and also show interest in other people's lives.

Transition Education Links

This poem links to objectives in Chapter 5, "Friendships and Relationships." Ask your students why the speaker feels sorry for Kate. Perhaps he or she senses her loneliness. Ask your students to describe a time they or members of their family reached out to someone who was new to help them feel welcome. Maybe they invited them for a play date or to dinner. Have them also share times someone reached out to them and how it made them feel. Encourage the children to be sensitive to the feelings and experiences of those who are new and explore ways they can help them settle in.

This poem also links to Chapter 6, "Problem-Solving Skills." Kate needed help in learning how to make new friends since she resorted to bragging to impress them. Brainstorm with your class ways that Kate could have tried to make new friends without bragging. For example, she might have asked someone for help in going through the lunch line and then sat with that person at lunch. She might also ask the students to share with her the things they like best about their school. Discuss ways your students have approached settling into a new place themselves.

IDEAS FOR CROSS-CURRICULAR CONNECTIONS

Creative and Performing Arts

When people are moving back to an area where they have lived before, their minds begin to think of how the area looked when they lived there before. Often our memories paint actual pictures in our minds of buildings, landmarks, and geographical points. Whether you have many students moving back home or just one, plan a "memory art" lesson where each person in your class (including yourself) draws, sketches, or even paints from memory a picture of a definitive object back home. This object could be the building in which they lived or the school they attended. Other ideas might include a particular scene they saw each day, like a certain tree they admired or a storefront they passed daily on the way home. Then dedicate one wall of your classroom as a "gallery wall," and hang everyone's memory artwork there, complete with a small card giving the title of the artwork, the artist's name, and the place it depicts. Invite another class to come and tour your gallery's "opening."

Social Studies

Most of us have daily access to news from all over the world, and many teachers set aside one day of the week to discuss current events in their social studies classes. Extend that idea by giving your students a weekly or monthly assignment of finding out some current events about the home country they are returning to. Information can come from the newspaper, a magazine, the Internet, or even television or radio. Show students how to be a discriminating reporter by stating just the facts: who, what, when, where, how, and why. Talk ahead of time about the sensationalism of the news and how not all newsworthy stories report happy news.

Science and Technology

Link your students' experience of moving back to a technology project. Have them use the Internet to find information about the place they are moving back to and see how it may have changed from when they lived there. They can E-mail friends and relatives with their questions about popular movies, toys, and other current trends. They can also learn to create a Web site as a way to keep in touch with all the friends they have made in their present location.

Math

You can help your students' understanding of fractions by helping them create a pie chart of all the places they have lived, and then help them to convert that pie chart into equivalent fractions. Give students a template of a large circle and have them write their age in years at the top of the paper. Then along the side of the paper have them list all the different places they have lived in their lifetime with their corresponding ages. Demonstrate this by showing them how a pie chart would look for a 10-year-old who lived in Japan from birth to 3, England from 3 to 5, Cairo from 5 to 8, and Amsterdam from 8 to 10. Help them think of the pie chart in terms of a clock face that is being divided into 10 segments for their 10 years of life. To complete this activity, you can pair nonmobile students with students who have moved.

Cross-Referenced Literature and Transition Links

Books	The Common Experience of Mobility (Chapter 2)	The Process of Transition (Chapter 3)	Personal and Cultural Identity (Chapter 4)	Friendship and Relationships (Chapter 5)	Problem Solving Skills (Chapter 6)	Moving Back (Chapter 7)
Alexander, Who's Not (Do you hear me? I mean it!) Going to Move (Voirst)	•	✓		•	•	
Amber Brown Is Not a Crayon (Danziger)	•	•	•	✓	•	
Best Friends Together Again (Aliki)		•		✓	•	
Beyond the Mango Tree (Zemser)		•		✓	•	
Bloomability (Creech)	✓	•	•	•	•	•
Chicken Sunday (Dolacco)			•	•	✓	
Chrysanthemum (Henkes)				•	✓	
Dandelions (Bunting)	•	✓		•	•	
Gila Monsters Meet You at the Airport (Sharmat)	✓	•				
Going Home (Bunting)	•		•			✓
Grandfather's Journey (Say)	•		✓			•

Books	The Common Experience of Mobility (Chapter 2)	The Process of Transition (Chapter 3)	Personal and Cultural Identity (Chapter 4)	Friendship and Relationships (Chapter 5)	Problem Solving Skills (Chapter 6)	Moving Back (Chapter 7)
In the Year of the Boar and Jackie Robinson (Lord)		✓	•	•		
Ira Says Goodbye (Waber)		•		•	✓	
The Kid in the Red Jacket (Park)	•			✓	•	
little blue and little yellow (Lianni)		•	✓	•		
The Lotus Seed (Garland)					✓	
Mrs. Katz and Tush (Polacco)			•	✓		
Molly's Pilgrim (Cohen)					✓	
A New Home for Tiger (Stimson)	✓	•		•		
Painted Words and Spoken Memories (Aliki)	✓	•	•	•	•	
Sarah, Plain and Tall (MacLachlan)	✓	•		•		
Scrumpy (Dole)	•	✓				
Seedfolks (Fleischman)			✓			
Stellaluna (Cannon)		•	✓			
Tea with Milk (Say)						✓
"They Don't Do Math in Texas" (Dakos)				•		✓
The Trip Back Home (Wong)						✓
We Are Best Friends (Aliki)		✓		•		
When Africa Was Home (Williams)		•	•			✓
When I Was Young in the Mountains (Rylant)	•		✓			

✓   = Lesson plan in this chapter
•   = Transition links

Children's Literature Resources

There is a wealth of excellent children's literature available that easily lends itself to addressing transition issues and integrating transition education into the curriculum. Picture books have far-reaching appeal and can be used across all grade levels. These are titles we think are particularly useful. The titles marked with an asterisk (*) are those featured with lesson plans in this book.

Ajmera, M., & Ivanko, J. D. (1999). *To be a kid*. Watertown, MA: Charlesbridge.

*Aliki. (1982). *We are best friends*. New York: Greenwillow Books.

*Aliki. (1995). *Best friends together again*. New York: Greenwillow Books.

*Aliki. (1998). *Painted words and spoken memories*. New York: Greenwillow Books.

Asch, F. (1986). *Goodbye house*. New York: Aladdin Paperbacks.

Baer, E. (1990). *This is the way we go to school: A book about children around the world*. New York: Scholastic.

Brown, L. K., & Brown, M. (1998). *How to be a friend: A guide to making friends and keeping them*. New York: Little, Brown.

Bunting, E. (1988). *How many days to America?* Boston, MA: Houghton Mifflin.

*Bunting, E. (1995). *Dandelions*. Orlando, FL: Harcourt Brace.

*Bunting, E. (1996). *Going home*. New York: HarperCollins.

*Cannon, J. (1993). *Stellaluna*. New York: Harcourt Brace.

Cha, D. (1996). *Dia's story cloth*. New York: Lee & Low Books.

*Cohen, B. (1983). *Molly's pilgrim*. New York: William Morrow.

*Creech, S. (1998). *Bloomability*. New York: HarperCollins.

*Dakos, K. (1990). They don't do math in Texas. In *If you're not here, please raise your hand* (pp. 17–21). New York: Simon & Schuster.

*Dale, E. (1997). *Scrumpy*. London: Anderson Press.

*Danziger, P. (1994). *Amber Brown is not a crayon*. New York: Putnam & Grosset Group.

De Zutter, H. (1993). *Who says a dog goes bow-wow?* New York: Delacorte Press.

Dooley, N. (1991). *Everybody eats rice*. Minneapolis, MN: Carolrhoda Books.

Dooley, N. (1996). *Everybody bakes bread*. Minneapolis, MN: Carolrhoda Books.

*Fleischman, P. (1997). *Seedfolks*. New York: HarperCollins.

Fox, M. (1985). *Wilfred Gordon McDonald Partridge*. Brooklyn, NY: Kane/Miller.

Fox, M. (1997). *Whoever you are*. New York: Harcourt Books.

Friedman, I. R. (1984). *How my parents learned to eat*. New York: Houghton Mifflin.

*Garland, S. (1993). *The lotus seed*. New York: Harcourt Brace.

Gray, N. (1988). *A country far away*. London: Andersen Press.

Hamanaka, S. (1994). *All the colors of the earth*. New York: William Morrow.

Heine, H. (1997). *Friends*. New York: Aladdin Paperbacks.

*Henkes, K. (1991). *Chrysanthemum*. New York: Greenwillow Books.

Jiminez, F. (1998). *La mariposa*. New York: Houghton Mifflin.

Johnston, T. (1985). *The quilt story*. New York: Putnam.

Levine, E. (1989). *I hate English!* New York: Scholastic.

*Lionni, L. (1959). *little blue and little yellow*. New York: Mulberry Books.

*Lord, B. B. (1984). *In the year of the boar and Jackie Robinson*. New York: HarperCollins.

McGeorge, C. (1994). *Boomer's big day*. San Francisco: Chronicle Books.

*MacLachlam, P. (1985). *Sarah, plain and tall*. New York: HarperCollins.

MacLachlan, P. (1995). *What you know first*. New York: HarperCollins.

Moss, M. (1995). *Amelia's notebook*. Middleton, WI: Pleasant Company Publications.

Nicola-Lisa, W. (1994). *Bein' with you this way*. New York: Lee & Low Books.

*Park, B. (1987). *The kid in the red jacket*. New York: Random House.

Polacco, P. (1988). *The keeping quilt*. New York: Aladdin Paperbacks.

*Polacco, P. (1992). *Chicken Sunday*. New York: Putnam & Grosset Group.

*Polacco, P. (1992). *Mrs. Katz and Tush*. New York: Bantam Doubleday Dell Publishing Group.

Polacco, P. (1996). *The trees of the dancing goats*. New York: Simon & Schuster.

Rosen, M. (1992). *Elijah's angel*. New York: Voyager Books.

Rosen, M. (1993). *Moving*. New York: Penguin Books.

*Rylant, C. (1982). *When I was young in the mountains*. New York: Penguin Books.

*Say, A. (1993). *Grandfather's journey*. New York: Houghton Mifflin.

*Say, A. (1999). *Tea with milk*. New York: Houghton Mifflin.

Sharmat, M. W. (1978). *Mitchell is moving*. New York: Aladdin Paperbacks.

*Sharmat, M. W. (1980). *Gila monsters meet you at the airport*. New York: Aladdin Paperbacks.

*Stimson, J. (1996). *A new home for Tiger*. London: Scholastic Children's Books.

Thomas, S. M. (1998). *Somewhere today: A book of peace*. New York: Albert Whitman.

*Viorst, J. (1995). *Alexander, who's not (Do you hear me? I mean it!) going to move*. New York: Aladdin Paperbacks.

*Waber, B. (1988). *Ira says goodbye*. Boston: Houghton Mifflin.

Wells, R. (2001). *Yoko's paper cranes*. New York: Hyperion Books for Children.

*Williams, K. L. (1991). *When Africa was home*. New York: Orchard Books.

*Wong, J. S. (2000). *The trip back home*. New York: Harcourt.

*Zemser, A. B. (1998). *Beyond the mango tree*. New York: Greenwillow Books.

ACTIVITY BOOKS FOR CHILDREN

Baile, R. (1996). *We are moving*. Berkeley, CA: Tricycle Press.

Blohm, J. (1997). *Where in the world are you going?* Yarmouth, ME: Intercultural Press.

Davis, G. (1997). *The moving book: A kids' survival guide*. New York: Little, Brown.

Suggested Resources Related to Transition

Ender, M. G. (Ed.). (2002). *Military brats and other global nomads: Growing up in organization families.* London: Praeger.

Hayden, M., & Thompson, J. J. (Eds.). (1998). *International education: Principles and practice.* London: Kogan Page.

Hayden, M., & Thompson, J. J. (Eds.). (2000). *International schools and international education.* London: Kogan Page.

Jason, L., et al. (1992). *Helping transfer students.* San Francisco: Jossey-Bass.

Kohls, L. R. (1996). *Survival kit for overseas living.* Yarmouth, ME: Intercultural Press.

McCluskey, K. C. (Ed.). (1994). *Notes from a traveling childhood: Readings for internationally mobile parents and children.* Washington, DC: Foreign Service Youth Foundation.

Pollock, D. C., & Van Reken, R. E. (1999). *The third culture kid experience: Growing up among worlds.* Yarmouth, ME: Intercultural Press.

Sears, C. (1998). *Second language students in mainstream classrooms: A handbook for teachers in international schools.* Clevedon, England: Multilingual Matters.

Smith, C. D. (1991). *Absentee American: Repatriates' perspectives on America.* Bayside, NY: Aletheia Publications.

Smith, C. D. (Ed.). (1996). *Strangers at home: Essays on the effects of living overseas and coming "home" to a strange land.* Bayside, NY: Aletheia Publications.

Storti, C. (1990). *The art of crossing cultures.* Yarmouth, ME: Intercultural Press.

Storti, C. (1997). *The art of coming home.* Yarmouth, ME: Intercultural Press.

Taber, S. M. (1997). *Of many lands: Journal of a traveling childhood.* Washington, DC: Foreign Service Youth Foundation.

Transition Dynamics. *www.transition-dynamics.com*

Suggested Transition Activities

Provide activities for your students that help facilitate their arrival at and departure from your school. As arrival is a particularly sensitive time, be sure to choose activities that are culturally appropriate for each student. You and your class can create your own rituals.

For arriving students

- Assign a buddy to your new student.
- Explore the school and local neighborhood with the class.
- Introduce your new student to other teachers.
- Have your students make a welcome poster.
- Present your new student with a welcome bag with regional or school items such as pencils or erasers.

For departing students

- Have the class make a memory book for the child who is leaving, including poems, drawings, photographs, and good wishes.
- Have the class write good-bye cards.
- Sign a T-shirt or have a class-photo T-shirt made.
- Present the child with an appropriate gift from your country or school.
- Make a videotape of friends, the school, and favorite activities.
- Have the class record their good wishes and farewell thoughts on an audiotape.
- Have a good-bye party.
- Help the student complete a moving plan.
- Plan a miniunit for the class so everyone can learn something about where the departing child is going.

Approaches to Transition

These are useful ways to approach the many changes involved in moving:

- Plan ahead. Find out as much as possible about your new location.
- Reminisce with your family. It is important to remember people and places from your past.
- Know that it is okay to feel sad when you move.
- Know yourself and how you manage your feelings.
- Give yourself a break from worry and read a good book or watch a favorite movie.
- Develop rituals and traditions when you move.
- Bring your treasured objects with you when you travel to the new location.
- Develop a healthy curiosity about the new location or country.
- Ask questions.
- Take care of yourself; eat well, exercise, get plenty of rest, and make time to play or read.
- Keep in touch with friends and family.
- Find ways to do what you like to do in the new place.
- Realize things are done differently here.
- Be patient and flexible.
- Have a sense of humor.
- Make sure you say good-bye to people and places.
- Stay focused on the present as much as possible, and try not to worry about the past or future.
- Stop, look, and listen.
- Take risks by reaching out to others.
- Talk to friends and family about your feelings and concerns.
- Keep a journal to write or draw about your feelings.
- Have realistic expectations. Know the new place will be different.
- Accept a degree of uncertainty.

- If you are moving to another country, learn useful words and phrases in the new language.
- Observe cultural differences. Refrain from judgment and try to understand the way things are done in your new location.
- Take part in activities in the new culture.
- Explore new opportunities in the new country or state.

Tips for Parents

When teachers and parents work together, they can offer the most support to children in transition. These are suggestions to share with parents as they address transition issues with their family.

General suggestions

- Be flexible, patient, and have a sense of humor.
- Learn about the new location and have realistic expectations for the move.
- Recognize that the experience of transition is different for everyone and family members will all respond in their own way.
- Recognize that moving is stressful for everyone and that your children particularly need your love and support during this time.
- Acknowledge that moving is difficult, yet it can be made easier if you plan for it and know what to expect.
- Make sure you take care of yourself, as you will be dealing with your own transition issues as well as supporting your family.
- Children look to their parents as role models, and pick up on their attitudes. Try to remain as positive as possible, and demonstrate appropriate ways to manage stress and approach change.
- Provide familiar routines, and create and maintain family rituals.
- Include children in making choices and decisions where appropriate.
- Keep open and honest communication within the family, and set aside a time each day to check in with your child.
- Change causes stress. Make sure everyone eats well and gets plenty of rest and exercise.
- Plan ways for everyone to take a break from the stress and worry. Watch a favorite movie together or read a good book.
- Encourage your children to be patient, flexible, and have a sense of

humor. Let them know they will probably make some mistakes as they adjust to living in a new location, especially if it is a new culture as well.

- Help your children learn to accept a degree of uncertainty and try not to worry too much. It helps to stay focused on the present when unsure of what the future holds. Reassure them that no matter what happens, you are together as a family and will handle it.
- If it is a part of your family culture, engaging in spiritual practice during times of transition can bring strength and comfort.

Before the move

- Help your children learn as much as they can about the new location before moving there. If possible, share pictures of the new house, neighborhood, and school. Help your children have realistic expectations too.
- Help your children plan ways to say good-bye to the people, places, and things that were important to them. Make sure they have time to do so. Having closure is important in order to settle into the new place.
- Encourage your children to resolve any bad feelings or conflicts with others before leaving. Support them in finding ways to do this, as unresolved issues can stay with them.
- Talk with your children about the things they will miss and what they are concerned about. Allow your children to grieve and express their sad feelings. Also talk about what they are looking forward to.
- Help your children choose treasured objects to bring with them on the actual move itself.
- Arrange for the movers to pack your children's possessions last so they will be unpacked first. Having familiar things around them helps children feel more secure.
- Talk with your children about the reasons for the move. While this will not take away any sadness about the move, it will make it easier to accept.
- Read your children stories about moving, and provide books on moving for your children to read. There are also several moving activity books available.
- Let your children know things will be different and that it will take time to get used to the new place.
- Transfer school records as quickly as possible.

After arrival

- Plan family outings to have fun together and to explore the new location.
- Help your children find ways to do the activities they enjoy in the new place or when you move back home.

- Talk with your children about ways to choose and make new friends.
- Encourage your children to keep in touch with family and old friends through E-mail, phone calls, planned visits, or writing letters.
- Keep memories alive by reminiscing about your life abroad or in the last place you lived as a family. Ensure a balance between remembering the past and engaging in the present.
- Develop your own support system and network of friends in the new location.
- Find ways to engage with the local community.

SUGGESTIONS FOR MOVING BACK

For many children, moving to their passport country may be the first time they will live there and is like a move to another country. This is usually the most difficult transition, as people do not realize how much they have changed until they return home.

Before the move

- Talk with your children about moving back home. Let them know that it will be different than when they lived there before and that it will take time to adjust, just as it did when they moved abroad. Help them have realistic expectations.
- Explain to your school-age children that there will likely be gaps in their education because they will have learned different things in school abroad or in a different system. Encourage them to ask questions or explain this to their teachers. Reassure them that you will make sure they get whatever help they need.
- Talk with your children about how they have changed. Help them identify skills they have learned, knowledge they have gained, and new attitudes they may have. Encourage them to explore ways they can use these back home.
- If you are moving home from another country, link with other families who have lived abroad. Explore the availability of international clubs or organizations for your children and family.
- Set goals with your children for your arrival home. This may include finding a new soccer team or continuing music or language lessons.
- Help your children understand they will probably feel out of step with their peers for awhile.

- Talk with your child about the common experiences of returning to one's passport country. Help them to understand that it may take time to adjust to living in their own country.

After arrival

- Encourage your children to reestablish friendships and relationships back home. Let them know it takes time to reconnect with friends and family when you have been away.
- Talk with your children about sharing their experiences abroad or in the last place they lived a little at a time. Encourage them to show interest in others' lives as well.
- Look for signs of reentry shock. While they are natural, be aware of signs that persist over a prolonged period.

References

Bridges, W. (2001). *The way of transition*. Cambridge, MA: Perseus.

Jason, L., et al. (1992). *Helping transfer students*. San Francisco: Jossey-Bass.

Jasper, J. M. (2000). *Restless nation*. Chicago: University of Chicago Press.

Kids' random acts of kindness. (1994). Berkeley, CA: Conari Press.

Kohls, L. R. (1996). *Survival kit for overseas living*. Yarmouth, ME: Intercultural Press.

Langford, M. E. (1998). Global nomads, third culture kids and international schools. In M. Hayden & J. J. Thompson (Eds.), *International education: Principles and practice* (pp. 28–43). London: Kogan Page.

Langford, M. E. (1999). Observations on the mobile population of international schools. *International Schools Journal, 18*(2), 28–35.

McCaig, N. (1992). Birth of a Notion. *The Global Nomad Quarterly, 1*(1), 1–2.

McKillop-Ostrom, A. (2000). Student mobility and the international curriculum. In M. Hayden & J. J. Thompson (Eds.), *International schools and international education* (pp. 73–84). London: Kogan Page.

Pollock, D. C., & Van Reken, R. E. (1999). *The third culture kid experience: Growing up among worlds*. Yarmouth, ME: Intercultural Press.

Schaetti, B. (1998). Transitions resource teams: a good answer to an important question. *International Schools Journal, 17*(2), 52–58.

Useem, R. H. (1976). Third culture kids. *Today's Education, 65*(3), 103–105.

Useem, R. H., & Cottrell, A. B. (1996). Adult third culture kids. In C. D. Smith (Ed.), *Strangers at home: Essays on the effects of living overseas and coming "home" to a strange land* (pp. 22–35). Bayside, NY: Aletheia Publications.

Wertsch, M. E. (1991). Military brats as nomads. In M. E. Wertsch et al. (Eds.), *Military brats: Legacies of childhood inside the fortress*. New York: Harmony Press.

Wood, W. (1993). *Spirit walker*. New York: Doubleday.

Index

Activities. *See* Follow-up activities;
    Learning activities; Post-reading
    activities; Pre-reading activities
ADAPT model, 32–33, 41–43, 44–45,
    49, 53, 62–63, 106–107, 145
Adjustments of people who stay
    behind, 46–47, 50
*Alexander, Who's Not (Do you hear me?
    I mean it!) Going to Move* (Viorst),
    47–50
    follow-up activities, 49–50
    objectives, 48
    post-reading activities, 48–49
    pre-reading activities, 48
    synopsis, 47
    transition education links, 50
Aliki
    Best Friends Together Again, 93–95
    Painted Words and Spoken Memories
        (Aliki), 24–33
    We Are Best Friends, 58–60
Amber Brown is Not a Crayon
    (Danziger), 99–103
    follow-up activities, 101–102
    objectives, 99
    post-reading activities, 100–101
    pre-reading activities, 99
    synopsis, 99
    transition education links, 102–103
Assimilation, 70

Benefits and challenges of moving, 14,
    15, 22–23, 56

Best Friends Together Again (Aliki), 93–95
    follow-up activities, 95
    objectives, 93
    post-reading activities, 94–95
    pre-reading activities, 94
    synopsis, 93
    transition education links, 95
Beyond the Mango Tree (Zemser), 107–
    111
    during-reading activities, 108–109
    follow-up activities, 110–111
    objectives, 108
    post-reading activities, 109–110
    pre-reading activities, 108
    synopsis, 107–108
    transition education links, 111
Bloomability (Creech), 33–39
    discussion and reflection, 36–37
    follow-up activities, 36
    objectives, 34
    post-reading activities, 34–36
    pre-reading activities, 34
    synopsis, 33–34
    transition education links, 37–39
Bragging, 156–157
Bridges, William, 116
Bullying, 130
Bunting, Eve, 129
    Dandelions, 51–55
    Going Home, 150–153

Cannon, Janell, *Stellaluna*, 72–75
Carter, Rosalynn, 123–124

Chicken Sunday (Polacco), 117–121
  follow-up activities, 120
  objectives, 117
  post-reading activities, 118–120
  pre-reading activities, 117–118
  synopsis, 117
  transition education links, 120–121
Chrysanthemum (Henkes), 121–124
  follow-up activities, 123
  objectives, 121
  post-reading activities, 122–123
  pre-reading activities, 121–122
  synopsis, 121
  transition education links, 123–124
Classroom programs, 8
Classroom structure, 8–9
Closure process, 116–117, 132
Cohen, Barbara, *Molly's Pilgrim*, 128–
  131
Common experience of mobility, 13–
  40
  concepts featured in learning
    activities, 14–16
  cross-curricular connections, 39–40
  lesson plans, 16–39
  moving back, 138–139
  transition education links, 18–19,
    24, 28–29, 32–33, 37–38, 50, 54,
    58, 78, 81, 102, 106, 133, 144–
    145, 150, 153
  in transition education model, 4
Community building, 8
Cottrell, A. B., 3
Country Far Away, A (Gray), 145
Creative and performing arts, cross-
  curricular connections, 39–40, 65–
  66, 87, 112, 134, 159
Creech, Sharon, *Bloomability*, 33–39
Cross-cultural skills, 116, 119
Cross-curricular connections
  in common experience of mobility,
    39–40
  creative and performing arts, 39–40,
    65–66, 87, 112, 134, 159
  in friendships and relationships,
    112–113

mathematics, 40, 66–67, 88–89, 113,
  135, 160
in personal and cultural identity,
  87–89
science, 40, 66, 88, 112–113, 134–
  135, 160
social studies, 40, 66, 87–88, 112,
  134, 159–160
in transition process, 65–67
Cultural adaptation, 33, 43–44, 45–46,
  75
Cultural differences, 9–10, 11, 71–72,
  85, 91–92, 129
Cultural iceberg (Kohls), 68, 69
Cultural identity. *See* Personal and
  cultural identity
Culture shock, 9, 33, 42, 45–46, 52, 63,
  111, 133, 143, 148
  reverse, 137, 140, 143

Dakos, Kalli, "They Don't Do Math in
  Texas" (in *If You're Not Here,
  Please Raise Your Hand*), 156–159
Dale, Elizabeth, *Scrumpy*, 55–58
Dandelions (Bunting), 51–55
  follow-up activities, 53
  objectives, 51
  post-reading activities, 52–53
  pre-reading activities, 51–52
  synopsis, 51
  transition education links, 54–55

Danziger, Paula, *Amber Brown is Not a
  Crayon*, 99–103
During-reading activities, grade 5,
  108–109

Empathy, 28, 60, 92–93, 100, 105
Entering stage of transition, 42, 44–45
Extracurricular activities, 10
Eye contact, 68

Fleischman, Paul, *Seedfolks*, 83–87
Follow-up activities
  grade K–2, 18
  grade K–3, 60, 123

grade K–5, 28, 32, 49–50, 57, 78, 80,
    83, 95, 98, 126, 130, 133, 144,
    149, 153, 155, 158
grade 3–5, 23–24, 53, 101–102, 106,
    120
grade 4–5, 64–65, 86
grade 5, 36, 110–111
Food, trying new, 64, 66, 86, 88–89,
    155
Friendships and relationships, 90–113
    concepts featured in activities, 91–93
    cross-curricular connections, 112–113
    lesson plans, 93–111
    transition education links, 18–19,
        24, 28–29, 38–39, 50, 54, 60, 65,
        75, 83, 86–87, 95, 98–99, 102–
        103, 106–107, 120–121, 123–124,
        127, 130, 145–146, 158–159
    in transition education model, 4

Garland, Sherry, *The Lotus Seed*, 131–134
Gestures, 68
Gifts, 49, 155
Gila Monsters Meet You at the Airport
    (Sharmat), 29–33
    follow-up activities, 32
    objectives, 29
    post-reading activities, 30–32
    pre-reading activities, 29–30
    synopsis, 29
    transition education links, 32–33
Going Home (Bunting), 150–153
    follow-up activities, 153
    objectives, 150–151
    post-reading activities, 151–153
    pre-reading activities, 151
    synopsis, 150
    transition education links, 153
Grade levels. *See* Lesson plans
Grandfather's Journey (Say), 76–79
    follow-up activities, 78
    objectives, 76
    post-reading activities, 77–78
    pre-reading activities, 76–77
    synopsis, 76
    transition education links, 78–79

Gray, Nigel, 145
Grieving process, 3, 46, 59, 127, 138

Henkes, Kevin, *Chrysanthemum*, 121–
    124
Home, concept of, 14, 16, 137, 142,
    152–153
Home language and culture, 12, 70,
    97. *See also* Moving back
Honeymoon period, 42, 45, 137
How Many Days to America (Bunting),
    129

Identity. *See* Personal and cultural
    identity
Interest Inventories, 8
Interpersonal skills, 116
*In the Year of the Boar and Jackie
    Robinson* (Lord), 61–65
    follow-up activities, 64–65
    objectives, 61
    post-reading activities, 62–64
    pre-reading activities, 61–62
    synopsis, 61
    transition education links, 65
Involvement stage of transition, 41, 44
Ira Says Goodbye (Waber), 124–127
    follow-up activities, 126
    objectives, 124
    post-reading activities, 125
    pre-reading activities, 124–125
    synopsis, 124
    transition education links, 126–127

Jason, L., 3
Jasper, J. M., 3

Kid in the Red Jacket, The (Park), 103–107
    follow-up activities, 106
    objectives, 103–104
    post-reading activities, 104–106
    pre-reading activities, 104
    synopsis, 103
    transition education links, 106–107
Kids' Random Acts of Kindness, 123–124
Kohls, L. Robert, 68, 69

Langford, Mary E., 3
Language
    language differences, 21
    learning new language, 35, 38, 61,
        64
    working with second language
        learners, 12
Learning activities, 8, 167. *See also*
        Follow-up activities; Post-reading
        activities; Pre-reading activities
    ADAPT model, 62–63
    advice columns, 102
    ambassadorship, 61–62, 63
    audiotape preparation, 95
    bio-sketches, 96–98
    blueprints of last house, 18
    board game design, 134
    book writing and publishing, 80
    brainstorming, 26, 28, 33, 39, 49, 51–
        52, 100, 125, 130–131
    bulletin boards, 101–102
    cause and effect chart, 52, 53
    characteristics of friends, 108
    character lists, 48, 84–85
    charting differences and
        similarities, 109
    Color Memory Mural, 54
    cultural passports, 103
    Cultural Sharing Day, 82–83
    cultural traditions list, 98
    descriptive writing, 36
    discussion and reflection, 36–37
    double entry diary, 50
    dramatic reading or role-playing, 158
    drawing sights and sounds, 153
    emotions lists, 48
    feelings questionnaire, 57
    friendship collage, 112
    garden/plants, 84, 112
    Harvest Festival, 86
    Interest Inventory, 8
    International Day, 83
    International Feast, 86
    International Games Day, 83
    International Music Festival, 134
    interviews, 49

journal-writing, 49, 78, 112, 120
language-learning, 35
letter-writing, 35, 36, 52–53, 60, 64–
    65, 105, 112
map skills, 40, 66, 77
memory charts, 20, 21
memory passports, 144
misconceptions and stereotypes, 31
mobiles, 37
nameplates, 61–62, 123
Our Special Memories videotape, 27
Painted Words Wall, 27
paper kites, 155
patterned books, 18
photo collage, 80
photo essays, 18
pictorial maps of personal history,
    35
picture walk, 49
poetry writing, 23–24, 36, 65, 95, 155
reaching out to others, 104
readers' theatre, 101
sense memories, 142, 143
sensory words, 26–27, 80
Sequence Triangle, 146–148
sharing own experiences, 55–56, 57,
    76–77, 79, 82–83, 99, 104
social skills learning, 63–64
Spoken Memories Wall, 27
strategies for moving, 31–32, 32, 46,
    102
"Ten Things I Loved Best about
    Living in _____," 145
time line, 53
time zones, 135
Tips for Moving class book, 24, 26
treasured objects, 21, 132
"Twenty Things I Like to Do," 59
Venn diagrams, 21, 22, 82, 100
Welcome Book, 130
When_____Was Home books, 144
worries and concerns for moving,
    14, 22–23, 26, 30, 121–122
writing graduation speech, 36
writing *The Big Move*, 34
Learning styles, 7

Leaving stage of transition, 41–42, 44,
    127
Lesson plans. *See also names of specific
    books*
    grade K–2, 16–19
    grade K–3, 58–60, 121–124
    grade K–5, 24–33, 47–50, 72–83, 93–
        99, 124–134, 141–159
    grade 3–5, 19–24, 51–55, 99–107,
        117–121
    grade 4–5, 61–65, 83–87
    grade 5, 33–39, 107–111
Lionni, Leo, *little blue and little yellow*,
    81–83
little blue and little yellow (Lionni), 81–83
    follow-up activities, 83
    objectives, 81
    post-reading activities, 82–83
    pre-reading activities, 81–82
    synopsis, 81
    transition education links, 83
Lord, Bette Bao, *In the Year of the Boar
    and Jackie Robinson* (Lord), 61–65
Lotus Seed, The (Garland), 131–134
    follow-up activities, 133
    objectives, 131
    post-reading activities, 132–133
    pre-reading activities, 131–132
    synopsis, 131
    transition education links, 133–134

MacLachlan, Patricia, *Sarah, Plain and
    Tall*, 19–24
Mathematics, cross-curricular
    connections, 40, 66–67, 88–89,
    113, 135, 160
McCaig, Norma, 2
McKillop-Ostrom, A., 4
Memories of people and places, 14–
    15, 16, 40
Military families, 3
Mobility. *See also* Common experience
    of mobility; *entries beginning with*
    "Transition"
    impact on friendships, 92
    research on, 2, 3

Modeling, 7, 75
Molly's Pilgrim (Cohen), 128–131
    follow-up activities, 130
    objectives, 128
    post-reading activities, 128–130
    pre-reading activities, 128
    synopsis, 128
    transition education links, 130–131
Money, 66–67
Moving back, 136–160
    concepts featured in activities, 138–
        141
    cross-curricular connections, 159–
        160
    lesson plans, 141–159
    as most difficult transition, 136–138
    stages of, 137
    transition education links, 39, 78–
        79
    in transition education model, 4
Mrs. Katz and Tush (Polacco), 96–99
    follow-up activities, 98
    objectives, 96
    post-reading activities, 97–98
    pre-reading activities, 96–97
    synopsis, 96
    transition education links, 98–99

Name calling, 129, 130
New Home for Tiger, A (Stimson), 16–
    19
    follow-up activities, 18
    objectives, 16
    post-reading activities, 17–18
    pre-reading activities, 17
    synopsis, 16
    transition education links, 18–19

Painted Words and Spoken Memories
    (Aliki), 24–33
    follow-up activities, 28
    objectives, 25
    post-reading activities, 25–28
    pre-reading activities, 25
    synopsis, 24–25
    transition education links, 28–29

Parents, working with, 11
Park, Barbara, *The Kid in the Red Jacket*, 103–107
Personal and cultural identity, 68–89
    concepts featured in activities, 71–72
    cross-curricular connections, 87–89
    lesson plans, 72–87
    transition education links, 28, 38, 65, 74–75, 78–79, 81, 83, 86–87, 98–99, 102–103, 120, 130, 134, 145, 150, 153
    in transition education model, 4
Polacco, Patricia
    Chicken Sunday, 117–121
    Mrs. Katz and Tush, 96–99
Pollock, David C., 2–3, 41, 115, 126
Post-reading activities
    grade K–2, 17–18
    grade K–3, 59, 122–123
    grade K–5, 25–28, 30–32, 48–49, 56–57, 73–74, 77–78, 80, 82–83, 94–95, 97–98, 125, 128–130, 132–133, 142–144, 147–149, 151–153, 154–155, 157–158
    grade 3–5, 20–23, 52–53, 100–101, 104–106, 118–120
    grade 4–5, 62–64, 84–86
    grade 5, 34–36, 109–110
Pre-reading activities
    grade K–2, 17
    grade K–3, 58–59, 121–122
    grade K–5, 25, 29–30, 48, 55–56, 73, 76–77, 79–80, 81–82, 94, 96–97, 124–125, 128, 131–132, 142, 146–147, 151, 154, 156–157
    grade 3–5, 19, 51–52, 99, 104, 117–118
    grade 4–5, 61–62, 84
    grade 5, 34, 108
Problem-solving skills, 114–135
    concepts featured in activities, 116–117
    cross-curricular connections, 134–135
    lesson plans, 117–134

transition education links, 29, 39, 50, 55, 87, 95, 103, 107, 111, 156, 159
    in transition education model, 4
Professional development, 11–12

RAFT strategy, 115, 126
Readjustment, 137, 140
Reinvolvement stage of transition, 42, 45
Responses to moving, 45
Reverse culture shock, 137, 140, 143
Rylant, Cynthia, *When I Was Young in the Mountains*, 79–81

Sarah, Plain and Tall (MacLachlan), 19–24
    follow-up activities, 23–24
    objectives, 19
    post-reading activities, 20–23
    pre-reading activities, 19
    synopsis, 19
    transition education links, 24
Say, Allen
    Grandfather's Journey, 76–79
    Tea With Milk, 146–150
Schaetti, B., 4
Science, cross-curricular connections, 40, 66, 88, 112–113, 134–135, 160
Scrumpy (Dale), 55–58
    follow-up activities, 57
    objectives, 55
    post-reading activities, 56–57
    pre-reading activities, 55–56
    synopsis, 55
    transition education links, 58
Seating, 8
Second-language learners, 12
Seedfolks (Fleischman), 83–87
    follow-up activities, 86
    objectives, 84
    post-reading activities, 84–86
    pre-reading activities, 84
    synopsis, 83–84
    transition education links, 86–87
Sharmat, Marjorie Weinman, *Gila Monsters Meet You at the Airport*, 29–33

Skill development, 15

Social studies, cross-curricular connections, 40, 66, 87–88, 112, 134, 159–160

Spiritwalker (Walker), 7–8

Stellaluna (Cannon), 72–75
objectives, 73
post-reading activities, 73–74
pre-reading activities, 73
synopsis, 72
transition education links, 74–75

Stimson, Joan, *A New Home for Tiger*, 16–19

Teaching strategies, 7

Tea With Milk (Say), 146–150
follow-up activities, 149
objectives, 146
post-reading activities, 147–149
pre-reading activities, 146–147
synopsis, 146
transition education links, 150

"They Don't Do Math in Texas" (in *If You're Not Here, Please Raise Your Hand*) (Dakos), 156–159
follow-up activities, 158
objectives, 156
post-reading activities, 157–158
pre-reading activities, 156–157
synopsis, 156
transition education links, 158–159

Third Culture Kids (TCKs)
characteristics of, 3, 15–16, 37
defined, 2
identity and, 2
research on adult, 3

Transition
defined, 2
mobility research, 2, 3

Transition education
approaches to transition, 168–169
cultural differences in, 9–10
direct ways of addressing, 6–7
guidelines for working with mobile families, 9
indirect ways of addressing, 7–8

model for. *See* Transition education model

process of. *See* Transition process

professional development, 11–12
structuring classroom in, 8–9
working with children, 10–11
working with parents, 11
working with second language learners, 12

Transition education model, 3–4
Common Experience of International Mobility, 4, 13–40
Friendships and Relationships, 4, 90–113
Moving Back, 4, 136–160
Personal and Cultural Identity, 4, 68–89
Problem-Solving Skills, 4, 114–135
Process of Transition, 4, 41–67

Transition process, 41–67
concepts featured in learning activities, 43–47
cross-curricular connections, 65–67
lesson plans, 47–65
stages of, 2–3, 41–43, 44–45
transition education links, 18, 24, 28, 32–33, 37–38, 60, 65, 74–75, 83, 95, 102, 106–107, 111, 126–127, 133, 145
in transition education model, 4

Transition-related experiences, 7–8

Transition Resource Team, 11–12

Transition stage of transition, 42, 44

Traumatic circumstances, 9

Trip Back Home, The (Wong), 154–156
follow-up activities, 155
objectives, 154
post-reading activities, 154–155
pre-reading activities, 154
synopsis, 154
transition education links, 156

Useem, John, 2

Useem, Ruth H., 2, 3

Van Reken, R.E., 2–3, 41, 115
Viorst, Judith, *Alexander, Who's Not (Do you hear me? I mean it!) Going to Move*, 47–50

Waber, Bernard, *Ira Says Goodbye*, 124–127
Walker, Nancy, 7–8
Way of Transition, The (Bridges), 116
We Are Best Friends (Aliki), 58–60
  follow-up activities, 60
  objectives, 58
  post-reading activities, 59
  pre-reading activities, 58–59
  synopsis, 58
  transition education links, 60
Wertsch, M.E., 3
When Africa Was Home (Williams), 141–146
  follow-up activities, 144
  objectives, 141–142

post-reading activities, 142–144
pre-reading activities, 142
synopsis, 141
transition education links, 144–146
When I Was Young in the Mountains (Rylant), 79–81
  follow-up activities, 80
  objectives, 79
  post-reading activities, 80
  pre-reading activities, 79–80
  synopsis, 79
  transition education links, 81
Williams, Karen Lynn, *When Africa Was Home*, 141–146
Wong, Janet S., *Trip Back Home, The*, 154–156
Worries and concerns for moving, 14, 22–23, 26, 30, 121–122, 142–143

Zemser, Amy Bronwen, *Beyond the Mango Tree*, 107–111

About the Authors

Debra Rader earned a B. S in clementary education at Keene State College in New Hampshire, and a M. Ed. in Instructional Leadership from the University of Illinois at Chicago. Part of her graduate work was undertaken at the University of Bath in England, in the field of International Education. Debra has extensive teaching experience at both the primary and middle school levels in the United States and abroad. She has taught in the Fayette County Schools (Kentucky), at Hampstead International School (London), in Arlington and Fairfax County Schools (Virginia), and at the Latin School of Chicago. Debra was also primary and middle school principal at Southbank International School Kensington in London.

Debra became interested in the area of transitions through her work with internationally mobile children and their families. She developed a model for transition education and materials for educators using children's literature as a springboard to address transition issues in the classroom. She conducts transition workshops for educators and parents at international schools and conferences worldwide. Debra recently returned to the classroom and is currently teaching at Southbank International School Hampstead in London. She lives in London with her husband, Jim.

Linda Harris Sittig was born in Greenwich Village in New York City and moved as a young child to suburban New Jersey. After earning a B. A. at Grove City College in Pennsylvania, she then completed a M. Ed. at Bowie University in Maryland. Linda's first exposure to transition and international living was as a university student in Lausanne, Switzerland. When she returned to the States she began her teaching career with the goal of helping students become lifelong readers and writers.

Linda currently teaches in a public school in Fairfax County, Virginia, where the student body hails from 46 different countries and student mobility is a daily issue. She is also a graduate school adjunct professor at Shenandoah University in Winchester, Virginia, and was named the Virginia State Reading Teacher of the Year in 1983 and the International Elementary Language Arts Teacher of the Year in 1993. Linda lives with her husband, Jim, near the Blue Ridge Mountains; their twin daughters, Jamie and Jennie, are now grown.